A Background
for Domenico Scarlatti

DOMENICO SCARLATTI

A Background for Domenico Scarlatti

1685–1757

*written for his
two hundred and fiftieth
anniversary
by*

Sacheverell
Sitwell

*ML
410
S221
558*

GREENWOOD PRESS, PUBLISHERS
WESTPORT, CONNECTICUT

Originally published in 1935
by Faber and Faber Ltd., London

First Greenwood Reprinting 1970

Library of Congress Catalogue Card Number 74-109776

SBN 8371-4335-7

Printed in the United States of America

To
Violet Gordon Woodhouse
scholar and pupil
of
Scarlatti

Contents

★

i
Introduction

★

THE SUBJECT OF THESE PAGES IS A PROBLEM
to be approached with temerity. There is, perhaps, no other artist of a comparable importance about whom so little has been attempted.
The reasons for this silence are not difficult to
seek. First of all, practically nothing is known of
Domenico Scarlatti except the mere dates of the
main periods in his life. He was in Naples, or in
Rome, or in Madrid, for ten years, and there
our information ends. Neither is there any body
of his correspondence in existence; indeed, no
more than two or three unimportant letters
from him have survived. An Englishman, Dr.
Burney, is the chief source of information on a
subject upon which there is little more than

an embarrassed silence, both in Italy and in Spain.

Another reason for this lack of comment is that, in another sense, also, there is nothing to say. For the hundreds of pieces that Scarlatti wrote differ profoundly from each other, but are all conceived in the same form. They are not even known by picturesque titles, as was the case with the harpsichord pieces of Couperin and Rameau. Scarlatti's sonatas are entirely lacking in this convenience of discussion. And it may be thought that even the most enthusiastic admirer of Scarlatti would quail before a purely technical examination of nearly six hundred pieces of almost similar length, with no titles by which to distinguish them from each other. Nor has this ever been attempted, for it is a task that is obviously impossible to accomplish. So we see that the combination of these two things, lack of information, and what we might term absence of landmark, have contrived this deep and lasting silence upon the one old Italian master whose works are still a part of the public pleasure.

Introduction

But, first of all, let us confirm his stature. As composer, the concentration of his energies upon one instrument alone is a peculiarity that places him upon the same eminence as Chopin. No two artists could be more different from each other in temperament, but they are allied in this respect that they composed only for the one instrument. The association of their names is no derogation of each other. Perhaps, in the case of Scarlatti, the range of his genius is even more astonishing because of the immense variety of expression, of atmosphere, with which he was able to invest the one form, and the one form only, upon which he lavished all the wealth of his invention. These short pieces, hardly ever exceeding two or three minutes in length, are admirable in their expression of different moods. No one, as we have said, could be more different from Chopin, and the mention of his name is only in order to establish the stature of Scarlatti beside him. It would, indeed, be more easy to compare Scarlatti with Liszt; the breath of virtuosity is common to both in a sense in which it is not to be found in Chopin. It is, of course, the reflection of Scarlatti's inordinate skill as a performer.

For the importance of Domenico Scarlatti from the executive side is that he was the finest player of the harpsichord who ever lived. The evidence of Handel must be accepted as conclusive as to this. None of the other great musicians were specialists in this branch of their art. We may believe the highest surmises of Bach's playing, or the direct reports of Mozart's skill and invention, but in each case this instrument was only a part, only a facet of their accomplishment. Until the appearance of Liszt, Domenico Scarlatti was the greatest virtuoso in history.

There are reasons for this aspect in his music that can be referred directly to the circumstances of his life. So few of his compositions were published in his lifetime that it can never have been in his interest to simplify their ornament for the sake of an inexperienced player. His music was written for his own performance alone, and so it retains the marks of his personality to a degree that is without a parallel in piano music until we come, after the lapse of a

Introduction

century, to the earliest of the parade pieces of
Liszt. In these, also, virtuosity is an end in itself. The music, both of Scarlatti and of Liszt,
requires the highest degree of skill on the part
of the performer. And yet there is, of course,
much more than the mere lapse of a century
between Scarlatti and Liszt. If they meet on
ground of mutual virtuosity, they are but remotely related to each other in inspiration and
subject. This is because Scarlatti wrote only for
himself and for his private patrons. It is, therefore, music of a quite different intention from
the pyrotechnics of Liszt, even if the pheno-
menal brilliance of its author gives it some
points of resemblance to Liszt, while his fertility of resource, the manifold variety of his
imagination, makes him a figure comparable to
Chopin.

Scarcely any of his pieces were engraved in
his lifetime,[1] but amateurs collected copies of
all the manuscripts that were available. The

[1]Domenico Scarlatti only published one book, *Eser-
cizii per gravicembalo*, dedicated to the Prince of the
Asturias, and printed in Venice, before 1746.

Introduction

Abbé Santini (1778-1862) possessed, so we are told, no fewer than three hundred and forty-nine original pieces, or sonatas, by Scarlatti. In the course of time, with the deaths of all who had heard him play, his music must have faded altogether from knowledge. It is significant that we owe its revival to the enthusiasm of Liszt, who first drew the attention of the public to it and headed the subscription for the edition of two hundred of his Sonatas edited by Czerny, in Vienna, in 1839. But a cult of Scarlatti had always been alive to some little extent in Vienna, it would seem, for Dr. Burney, the chief authority upon Scarlatti, bases most of his information upon details supplied to him by various persons whom he was lucky enough to meet in Vienna. Chief of these was a Dr. L'Augier, who had been Scarlatti's physician in Madrid. But this was in 1772, and by the 'thirties of the next century, the circle of Scarlatti admirers must have been nearly extinct in Vienna. To Liszt must go the initial credit for this rediscovery, and the edition of 1839 is appropriately dedicated to him. It is only since 1910 that all or

Introduction

nearly all of Scarlatti's music has been made available by the publication, by Alessandro Longo, of the complete edition of his sonatas, five hundred and forty-five in number, in eleven volumes.

Having established the stature and importance of our hero with a few general remarks upon his position in music, it is necessary to descend to particulars. The precise information that is available upon Scarlatti would cover only some couple of pages. In the absence of more details our object must be so to illuminate his background, or environment, that it becomes more easy to appreciate the exceptional character of all that he attempted. For it is this very lack of information that makes him so fascinating a subject. It is not an easy problem. The only possible solution of its difficulties lies in attention to his music and in the correct colouring of his surroundings. And this will have the added attraction of 'eading us into some of the most curious recesses in history. It will be a world which we might call a locked cabinet of taste.

Introduction

A long-standing interest in the neglected history of the Two Sicilies, Spain and Portugal, during this period is our excuse for attempting a task that could have been better achieved in other directions by a more professional hand. It is possible, though, that more expert guidance would be less sympathetic to these forgotten figures. But it would be a pity to introduce them at this point, and they must wait their time, when, perhaps, the information that is given about them will serve to form a fresh opinion of their merits and to explain, by this new colouring of his background, those unique and inimitable characteristics that belong to Domenico Scarlatti—and to him alone.

ii

Naples

★

THE RISE OF THE CURTAIN SHOWS THE MEDI-
terranean. But the sparkle of its waves is thrown
heedlessly upon the day, for no one has eyes for
its glitter. The shores, that are crowded with
fishermen and *lazzaroni*, are as bare in this
sense as virgin sands of an untrodden isle. In
fact, the sea is playing not to an empty theatre,
but to an audience who persist in looking away
from the stage and up into the boxes. This is
because all the houses in the town are built for
shade, and have, therefore, blind or shuttered
windows towards the sea. It is, of course,
Naples; as we can tell from the voices singing in
the crowd, and all over the town.

This ageless city is in the full ferment of its

Naples

febrile activities. It is the metropolis of the South: the one huge, perennial town of the South: this is the impression of anyone who looks out over Naples from a balcony or belvedere. Not only this, but at the time of which we are writing there were only two other towns in the whole of Europe to compare with Naples in point of population. These were London and Paris. Rome, a city of monks and nuns, was in little danger of a swarming in its streets: Venice was in decrepitude: the one great town of Italy was Naples. This has to be established as undisputed fact before we disclose in which year we are listening to its voices. For a confused babel of sound rises from the town; there are tenors singing in every street, and their songs are broken and interrupted by the cries of stall-vendors and by the chanting of religious processions. Santa Lucia swarms with people eating oysters and macaroni; fiddlers and harpers play at will on the Molo; even the placid waters of the bay carry back the tinkle of the guitar. It is, indeed, the kingdom of music. And now we may admit that the year is 1685; and that the reason for this choice of date is because it is the birth year of that person with whose activities we now propose to concern ourselves.

This is what Dr. Burney says of Naples, a century later, in his *Musical Tour*: 'It was at Naples only that I expected to have my ears gratified with every musical luxury and refinement that Italy could afford. My visits to other places were in the way of business, for the performance of a task that I had assigned myself; but I came hither animated with the hope of pleasure. And what lover of music could be in the place which had produced the two Scarlattis, Leonardo Leo, Pergolesi, Porpora, Farinelli, Jommelli, Piccinni, Traetta, Sacchini, and innumerable others of the first eminence among composers and performers, both vocal and instrumental, without the most sanguine expectations? . . . In the manner of their executing music there is, at Naples, an energy and fire not to be met with elsewhere, perhaps, in the whole universe: it is so ardent as to border upon fury, and from this impetuosity of genius, it is common for Neapolitan composers, in a move-

Naples

ment which begins in a mild and sober manner, to set the orchestra in a blaze before it is finished. Like high-bred horses, they are impatient of the rein, and eagerly accelerate their motion to the utmost of their speed, as Dr. Johnson says that Shakespeare, in tragedy, is always studying for an occasion to be comic.'

Does not this passage throw light upon a dead and forgotten world? For the composers mentioned by Dr. Burney are, with the solitary exception of the younger Scarlatti, completely and entirely unknown to the modern world. And it is precisely with the younger Scarlatti, who was born at Naples on October 26, 1685, that we are now concerned. His father, Alessandro Scarlatti, a musician of wider talent and more imposing stature, belongs to the decay of Spanish magnificence just before the birth of the lighter and more elegant rococo. For Naples, under the rule of the Spanish Viceroys, presented, perhaps, a deeper and more finished epitome of sombre extravagance than could be found in Madrid or in Seville, but its airs of mourning were constantly broken and contradicted by the native high spirits and exuberance of the Neapolitans. The nobles, most of whom had only Norman and Aragonese blood in their veins, and all of whom may be said to have had a brother or a sister in the church, lived in a ceremonial gloom that was at odd contrast with the intrigue and vendetta of their concealed existences. Nor was this passionate nature confined only to those rich enough to gratify its whims, for the vitality of the poorer classes, uncurbed by rules and conventions of caste, found a direct outlet in exuberance of gesture, in the dramatic arts, and in gifts of improvisation. But, above all, in music.

Of their prowess in this art the elder Scarlatti is one of the most distinguished protagonists. He experimented in every known form of music, more especially in opera, and he has been credited with the invention of all the current language of classical music. He is, in fact, the greatest of Italian classical composers; but his music is completely and utterly unknown to our ears. This is a curious fate, it will be admitted, to befall an artist whose importance can only be established if we compare him with Vignola or with Bernini.

Although he was the glory of the Neapolitan school Alessandro Scarlatti was not born at Naples, but it is believed on no certain evidence that his birthplace was at Trapani, in Sicily, a town so distantly connected by land with the rest of Italy that, in its isolation, it compares with one of the harbours of the outer Hebrides. But Trapani was in direct sail with Naples, and it was to this town that Alessandro Scarlatti came to seek his fortune. He lived in Naples from 1684 till 1702, and, again, from 1709 till 1719. His son, Domenico, was seventeen years old when his father moved away to Florence, in 1702, and subsequently to Rome. The musical education of Domenico must have taken place, therefore, at Naples, in the midst of that school whose names Dr. Burney brandishes so tantalisingly before us. It is impossible at this distance of time to appraise their qualities, but as an indication of what may be lost to us in the total neglect of the Neapolitan school we may quote these words from Professor E. J. Dent's

Naples

Life of Alessandro Scarlatti: 'The best pupil of Alessandro Scarlatti, we may safely say, is Mozart. Almost all those characteristics of style that we are accustomed loosely to consider as essentially Mozartian, were learned by Mozart from the Italians of the preceding half-century. Indeed, Mozart to some extent repeated the work of Scarlatti, uniting in himself the massive strength of Leo, the sweetness of Durante and Pergolesi, the swift energy of Vinci and the racy humour of Logroscino, together with that divine beauty of melody which belonged to Scarlatti alone.' Such were the different classes in the schooling, so to speak, of Domenico Scarlatti.

Not only the composing of music, but its performance, as well, was provided for, at Naples, as nowhere else. There is plenty of evidence as to this in the remarks of Dr. Burney, writing towards the end of the century. And, when reading the extracts that we are about to give, it must be remembered that the school of Naples was already in its decline at the time of Dr. Burney's visit. The youth of Domenico Scarlatti belongs to a period two generations before this, when the Neapolitan style was in its purity. At this earlier date, the greatest singers of all time were training at Naples. Farinelli, Cafarelli, Senesino, Egizziello, names that we shall meet with again in these pages, were the contemporaries of Domenico Scarlatti. All of these were Castrati, or male soprani, the products of a cruel operation, but the true reason for the glories of Italian opera down to the early days of Rossini.

The whole question of these Castrati singers is one of the most curious chapters in musical history. There can be no doubt that they were the most finished singers who have ever existed, and the few remarks upon their education in Dr. Burney are of great interest. He describes his visit to the Neapolitan conservatoires of music, and we shall read that he saw the Castrati in their dormitories, a vision not easily paralleled this side of the Seraglio and the Golden Horn. Not many of them were left, at that late day, but in their zenith during the youth of Scarlatti, the conservatoires of music were full to overflowing with unbudded aspirants.

Naples

These are Dr. Burney's words: 'This morning I went with young Oliver to his conservatorio of St. Onofrio, and visited all the rooms where the boys practise, sleep and eat. On the first flight of stairs was a trumpeter, screaming upon his instrument till he was ready to burst; on the second was a French horn, bellowing in the same manner. In the common practise-room was a Dutch concert, consisting of seven or eight harpsichords, more than as many violons, all performing different things and in different keys; other boys were writing in the same room; but, it being holiday time, many were absent who usually study and practise together.

'The beds, which are in the same room, serve for seats to the harpsichords, and other instruments. Out of thirty or forty boys that were practising, I could discover only two that were playing the same piece. . . . The violoncellos practise in another room; and the flutes, hautbois, and other instruments, in a third, except the trumpets and horns, which are obliged to fag either on the stairs, or on the top of the house.

[27]

Naples

'There are, in this College, sixteen young Castrati, and these lye upstairs, by themselves, in warmer apartments than the other boys, for fear of colds, which might not only render their delicate voices unfit for exercise at present, but hazard the entire loss of them for ever.

'The only vacation, in these schools, is in autumn, and that for a few days only; during the winter, the boys rise two hours before it is light, from which time they continue their exercise, an hour and a half at dinner excepted, till eight o'clock at night; and this constant perseverance for a number of years, with genius and good teaching, must produce great musicians.'

This amalgam of Dr. Squeer's Academy, the Seraglio, and the trumpet-factory, is described by Dr. Burney in words that bring it vividly before us. Later on, he gives us the results of his enquiries as to the manufacture of the Castrati. The practice was already frowned upon by authority, and most of them came from Lecce, in Apulia. This region, which is one of the great centres of rococo art, produced almost as many composers and singers as Naples itself, but their training invariably took place in the capital. Apulia, it may be supposed, was a little further removed from the writ of the law, so that the operation could be performed without the penalties attached to it in the capital. But Dr. Burney remarks that the number of Castrati with spoiled voices to be heard singing in church-choirs, and even in the streets, was proof of how seldom this barbarous mutilation succeeded in its purpose of preserving the voice.

Later on, in that same day, Dr. Burney presents us with another little scene which illustrates the abundance of good music at Naples. 'Having the honour, this day, of dining at our Minister's, I was very much entertained in the afternoon by the performance of a fat friar of the order of St. Dominic, who came there to sing *buffa* songs; he accompanied himself on the harpsichord in a great number of humorous scenes from the burletta operas of Piccinni and Paesiello, which he sang with comic force, little inferior to that of Casaccia, and with a much better voice.'

Naples

Such, at this time, was a day in that southern
city. For, above all, there was music at Naples.
This was the genius of that golden shore. Naples
was the name of music. This is what Jean-
Jacques Rousseau wrote in his *Dictionary of
Music* at the word Genius: 'Vas, cours, vole à
Naples.' The two things were synonymous in
his mind. Music was the art of Naples, just as
painting was the art of Venice. It is this that
we forget when we think of Naples.

That city was the musical centre of the
world, and the opening sentences of this chap-
ter are designed to draw attention to its peculiar
features. It is noticeable that its old houses are
built facing away from the incomparable view
over the Bay. The sea is described as playing,
not to an empty theatre, but to an audience
who persist in looking away from the stage and
up into the boxes. This is a way of saying that
the inhabitants are more interested in their internal affairs than in their external amenities.
It helps us in the delineation of Scarlatti to be
able to state that, like all true Neapolitans, he
was more interested in the animation of the

city than in the placid waters of the bay. Their
realist view of life makes the Neapolitans only
repair to the country for the *villeggiatura*, or
for a picnic on a saint's day. They only go to the
country for its coolness in the heat of summer,
not so much for its pretty sights as for its
advantages of air and breeze. For the rest of the
year, they are huddled together in houses built
as near to each other as possible. The only hour
of comparative silence is the siesta; the rest of
the day is a babel of voices, and noisiest of all
are the hours of night.

This is the metropolis of the South. At the
period of which we are speaking it had a full-
ness of life that can be compared to advantage
with the empty clatter of a modern city. Even
New York, which has at least its jazz-music,
the indigenous music of its streets, cannot vie
in point of proportion with what the richness of
visual and oral life must have been round the
Via de Toledo. This was the Broadway of old
Naples; and, while it had not the theatres and
cinemas of our age, the religious processions
and merely the spectators, were more pictur-

Naples

esque in their motley than all the cast of the screen, and even the entire company of the theatre thrown out and found upon the streets. We might cite, for instance, in the order in which they appeared, the different communities of monks and nuns, for Naples had a larger population of these celibates than any other city. There were Jesuits in their immense shovel-hats, like Don Basilio in *Barbiere*: Franciscans, shod or discalced: Dominicans, in the black and white from which they took their name: Carthusians, descended to the city from their Belvedere at San Martino, in white robes like Moors of Atlas: Oratorians of San Filippo Neri, black as their name: Trinitarians, with a cross of red upon black: white hermits of Camaldoli: monks of Monte Oliveto, whose pharmacy distilled the finest essences and compounded the most famous pomades of Naples: Benedictines, Servites, Capucins, Celestines, Theatines, all these and many more. The nuns, not less numerous; sisters of Santa Chiara, where the nuns were of noble birth, had each two serving maids, were never allowed out of the convent,

but received the best company in their salons
that gave upon a garden of trellised vines, above
benches of majolica tiles enamelled with
comedy-scenes; from the servitors of these princesses to mendicant Capucines in brown robes
and sandals, with wide hats of straw bound
tight to their faces with a wimple: and from
these vagrant nuns, who begged as they went,
to nuns of San Gregorio Armeno, magnificent
in black and red, and living in the most sump-
tuous rococo of all Naples. It was the preroga-
tive of these various orders of nuns to sell sweet-
meats of their own peculiar invention which
were prepared for set occasions, for a particular
season, some festival, a marriage-feast, or just
an ordinary dinner-party.[1] These confections of
chocolate or of orange-flower, these flavourings
of bergamot or lime, were diversified into a hundred different forms from the competition

[1]Instances of this practice are to be found all over
Italy. For instance, at Perugia, the nuns of Santa Lucia
were famed throughout the peninsula for their *pigno-
cate* and *ossa di morte*, little sugared cakes made in the
shapes of the different bones of a skeleton. Cf. Lalande,
Voyage en Italie, vol. vi, p. 270.

among so many convents; and the ices, the sorbets, and the sweets were called, even professionally, by names of a refreshing paganism.

If this was the religious pageantry of the streets in the city famous above all others in the world for processions and for festivals of saints, there was, also, the ever-playing fantasia of its beggars, unrivalled in lineage, for they had come down to the city from two thousand years of professional attendance. There were, also, the military; but, more striking than the soldiers, stood out from the crowd the unfortunate galley-slaves, who, marching in pairs, clanking their chains, passed under armed guard on their way to work. The different colour of their prison clothes proclaimed the crimes they had committed. Some wore blood-red, the colour of murder, some bright yellow, the colour of fraud and infamy. Thus, in their shame, they were paraded all through the streets.

As for the shops, it must be remembered that even now in the poorer quarter of Naples these are upon the oriental model, open to the streets, with a dark den serving as bedroom and living-

room at the back, and with all the bright colours
of the fruit and vegetables, the wax and tinsel
dolls of the religious shops, or the vividness of
cheap and glaring stuffs, all heaped indiscrimi-
nately where they could catch the light and
attract the passer-by. Next door to the blood-
stained horror of the butcher's shop would be a
shop full of melons and gourds, or with the
bladders of mozzarella, and macaroni in its
myriad shapes and sizes. In addition to this
vicarious colour of the town, it should be re-
marked that the peasants of Campania felix, of
the plain of Naples, wore costumes of a bewildering variety and rich golden jewellery of classical descent. Or, coming straight to the city
from the tall vines of the Capuan plain, they
wore the traditional white, the wine-stained
white of Pulcinella, discarded soon enough in
the summer when they worked naked in the
fields, or stood naked on ladders among the
trellised grapes as if the age of nudity, the
golden era of the statue, still existed. Goethe
described them, thus, on his visit to Italy, where
he saw that pagan vision of naked men, riding

horses into the sea. Not less unclothed were the *lazzaroni*, the lolling and mendicant beggars of the sea front, of whom there were no fewer than forty thousand at Naples; while fishermen and their women from Capri or from Ischia represented the canons of what we should at once recognise as one of the lost possibilities of modern art, being the exact personification of a phase of Picasso's genius, when his models were the classical women of the sea-shore, running along its strand, or posed with their creels of fish in still attitudes for the start of what should have been the greatest period of modern painting.

An erroneous view, which this context gives an opportunity to correct, would deny the presence of any considerable painters in Naples during the lifetime of Domenico Scarlatti. This is very far from being the truth. The defect of the Neapolitan school was that they were too exuberant to succeed upon a small scale. They were masters of fresco, not painters of easel pictures. The leading painter of the time was Solimena (1657-1747), and no person of un-

Naples

biassed taste who sees his frescoes of the Fall of
Simon Magus in the sacristy of S. Paolo
Maggiore, at Naples, will deny to Solimena a
very high place among the despised 'machinists'.
His masterpiece, perhaps, is the History of
Heliodorus, which fills a whole wall in the
gigantic church of the Gesù Nuovo; while other
good frescoes by his hand are those in the monastery church of Monte Cassino, and, again, in
a strangely inappropriate environment, in the
refectory of the convent at Assisi. His pupil
Francesco di Mura, known as Franceschiello, is a
painter of unrecognised merit. There is hardly
a church in Naples that does not contain his
works; but he is to be seen at his best at the
Certosa di S.Martino, above Naples. Sebastiano
Conca and Giuseppe Bonito are two more names
with which to contradict attacks upon Neapolitan painting. Frescoes by the former in the
church of S. Chiara, at Naples, and an extraordinary affair, the Probatica, or Pool of Siloam,
with pillars in trick perspective, in the chapel of
the Hospital of S.Maria della Scala, at Siena,
are witnesses to his skill. The Probatica, it may

[37]

be said, is about comparable to the frescoes by Hogarth in St. Bartholomew's Hospital.

As for contemporary architecture, at Naples, there was the great Ferdinando Sanfelice (1675-1750), who left his mark on Naples as did Fischer von Erlach upon Vienna. Sanfelice was the exact contemporary of Domenico Scarlatti. He excelled in designing the huge palaces which the nobles inhabited with all their married and unmarried relations; while his especial *forte* was the construction of double geometrical staircases. Two specimens of these are the Palazzo Serra Cassano, and his own palace, still called by his name, and containing two rooms which were decorated with the finest frescoes by Solimena in Naples. But they are, now, covered with whitewash, and even the memory of them has gone. Another good work by Sanfelice is his staircase in the monastery of S. Giovanni e Carbonara, with its library in the form of a star over a bastion. Sanfelice was poet and painter, as well as architect, and is known to have been musical. He must, beyond any reasonable doubt, have been acquainted with

Naples

Scarlatti. A city which held, simultaneously, two artists as energetic as Solimena and Sanfelice, apart from many lesser men of merit, cannot be accused of being lacking in the fine arts. Their handiwork is only the reasonable corollary to so much music.

We can leave Naples, indeed, with the assurance that there could be no better centre for the childhood and youth of a great musician. If its amenities have detained us at length it is because in such a case as that of Domenico Scarlatti, where so little is known about his life, the circumstances of his certain environment take on a decisive importance. It would be useless to mention Naples and not comment upon its music, where this was the soul of that city. If it is now forgotten, it is as if the whole body of Venetian painting had disappeared, leaving us only the names and none of the works. The fact that Domenico Scarlatti is the only survivor of his Italian age, even if no more than a piece or two of his composition is known to the average person, is, in itself, sufficient excuse for submitting this extension of his natal background.

iii
Venice

★

IT IS TIME NOW TO LEAVE NAPLES, AND IT was to Venice that Domenico Scarlatti proceeded, where he studied for a year under Gasparini and Bernardo Pasquini, in 1708. Venice was only second, as a centre of music, to Naples. And, perhaps, of both Naples and Venice at this time, no better description could be attempted than in a quotation from the Fourth Book of *The Dunciad*. The poet is describing an imaginary grand tour to the great cities of the arts:

To happy convents, bosomed deep in vines,
Where slumber abbots, purple as their wines:
To isles of fragrance, lily-silvered vales,
Diffusing languor in the panting gales:
To lands of singing, or of dancing slaves,
Love-whisp'ring woods, and lute-resounding waves.

[41]

Venice

But chief her shrine where naked Venus keeps,
And Cupids ride the lion of the deeps;
Where, eased of fleets, the Adriatic main
Wafts the smooth eunuch and enamoured swain.

The reading of these lines is like a magical
transition from the hot south up to Venice.
Capri and Ischia, isles of fragrance with their
cliffs of jonquil and narcissus, are evoked in the
same breath as Paestum in its plain of asphodel.
The poem, then, seems to move by magical
reptation through woods of ilex, as it might
be Rome evoked in its hills, to the decadence of Venice. That perpetual carnival is portrayed in the degradation of the lion of the
deeps, ridden by Cupids and garlanded with
flowers, while the venality of its decay is ex-
posed in the shrine of naked Venus. The last
couplet of all is a miraculous imagery of decrepitude, bringing, as it does, the tainted
waters of the Bosphorus to lap the marble quays
of Venice. The gliding caique is transposed for
the gondola; and then, in the next instant, the
voice of Senesino or Egizziello seems to sound,
though never named, upon the waters. Indeed,

after this, there is nothing to be said about Venice in its decadence. All, all is in that final couplet.

But, of his stay in Venice, there is at least one incident to report; and this brings Scarlatti into direct contact with a most interesting and neglected genius of our own race. Furthermore, it is described in the actual words of the narrator, as dictated by him to Dr. Burney. It concerns a certain Thomas Roseingrave, member of a family of musicians, and, perhaps, the most conspicuous instance of 'genius manqué' in the history of English music. Roseingrave was, at this time, some twenty years of age, and was studying in Italy. 'Being arrived at Venice on his way to Rome, as he himself told me,' writes Dr. Burney, 'he was invited as a stranger and a virtuoso, to an accademia at the house of a nobleman, where among others, he was requested to sit down to the harpsichord and favour the company with a toccata, as a specimen "della sua virtu". And, says he, finding myself rather better in courage and finger than usual, I exerted myself, my dear friend, and fancied by the applause I received, that my performance had made some impression on the company. After a cantata had been sung by a scholar of Gasparini, who was there to accompany her, a grave young man dressed in black with a black wig, who had stood in one corner of the room, very quiet and attentive while Roseingrave played, being asked to sit down to the harpsichord, when he began to play, Rosy said he thought ten hundred d——ls had been at the instrument; he never had heard such passages of execution and effect before. The performance so far surpassed his own, and every degree of perfection to which he thought he should ever arrive, that, if he had been in sight of any instrument with which to have done the deed, he would have cut off his own fingers. . . . Roseingrave declared he did not touch an instrument himself, for a month.' The young man dressed in black with a black wig was none other than Domenico Scarlatti, and so great was the impression he made upon Roseingrave that the latter, so to speak, attached himself to his person, accompanied him to Rome, and was seldom out of his company over a space of several years.

And we shall find in the course of this book that their friendship continued until a much later period, when a tragedy of melancholy clouded the brain of Roseingrave and left his genius unfulfilled.

Another friend, whose acquaintance he made during this visit to Venice, was Handel. He, also, had been studying under Gasparini, and was the exact contemporary of Scarlatti, having been born in the same year. They travelled, perhaps in each other's company, from Venice to Rome, and were to meet again, in subsequent years, in London. Handel was not far inferior to Scarlatti as a performer on the harpsichord, and so great was his admiration for Scarlatti that we are told the mere mention of his name, even in his very latest years, was sufficient to cause tears to come into his eyes. Scarlatti, for his part, was no less susceptible to the name of Handel, and would cross himself reverently, so we are told by Mainwaring, if Handel's name was brought into the conversation. In fact, this short stay in Venice must have marked an important stage in Scarlatti's life.

iv

Rome

*

WE COME TO ROME. DOMENICO SCARLATTI
lived here for ten years, from 1709 till 1719. In
the former year he entered the service of Queen
Marie Casimir of Poland, the widow of Sobieski,
then living in Rome, as composer to her private
opera. At this early period in his life he had
ambitions to follow in his father's career as a
composer of operas. He wrote, in fact, innumerable operas and cantatas during these ten years,
but must have become quickly convinced that
this was not his bent. In 1715 he was made
Maestro da cappella at St. Peter's, and had to
compose Masses and salve reginas as part of his
official employment. A more important influence upon him, however, was that of Cardinal

Rome

Ottoboni and his circle. Cardinal Pietro Ottoboni had been raised to the purple in 1690, an instance of the quick profits of nepotism, for his uncle, Alexander VIII, only reigned for the space of two years. The Cardinal was an enthusiastic amateur, who himself wrote operas, and was the patron of the Scarlattis, father and son, and of Handel. But, above all, this Cardinal was the protector of the great Corelli, who presided at weekly concerts of chamber-music every Monday, in the Cardinal's palace.[1] It is undeniable that this activity in the lesser fields of music must have been a great stimulus to Domenico Scarlatti. It is probable, indeed, that owing to Corelli, there was more chamber-music to be heard in Rome than in Naples. Rome, besides this, was several days' journey

[1]Arcangelo Corelli (1653-1713), a native of Imola, settled in Rome in 1685. He lived for nearly thirty years in the palace of his patron, Cardinal Ottoboni, gave weekly concerts, composed innumerable pieces of music, and collected pictures with the help of his friend Carlo Maratta. He left £60,000, the fruits of avarice, and his pictures, to the Cardinal, who accepted the pictures, but handed over the money to relatives.

[48]

nearer the rest of Europe than Naples; while the combination of its antiquities and its importance as seat of the Papacy drew all foreigners to Rome. There is every reason to think, then, that his ten years' stay in Rome was an important formative influence in his life and music.

Neither can the sensory effects of Rome be denied their bearing upon him. It would be impossible for any person of sensibility to remain ten years in Rome and not feel the force of that environment. Not for a moment is it necessary to assume that he had any archaeological interest in Roman ruins, but Rome as a centre of civilisation, past and present, as the perpetual fount, indeed, of civilisation, cannot fail to have left its impression upon any mind as neat and orderly, as civilised in the best sense of the word, and as full of imagination, as that of Scarlatti. Besides, we must remember that at the time of which we are speaking, the part of Rome which was not ruins was clean and new, and had not long issued from the builder's hands. To the kind of mind with which we are dealing this set of circumstances must always be a more inspiring background than the deadness of a countryside or the monotony of poverty. The Rome of Bernini was but just complete and the sparkle of its waters not yet jaded.

It was a town of some eighty thousand inhabitants, so that the smallness of the area that it occupied let it be overawed with magnificence by its buildings. All Rome lay between S. Maria degli Angeli and the Vatican, and it would be difficult to exaggerate the impression of so much energy spent on elegance and splendour. Instead of being the city of dust and beggars into which it had decayed at the fall of the Papacy, more than a hundred and fifty years later, Rome was the fine town of the modern world. We see this aspect of it whenever Piranese or Pannini stopped their extolling of its fallen columns in order to paint the present world before their eyes.

Let us depict, from Pannini (for the subject has a future importance to Scarlatti), the Piazza of St. Peter's during the arrival of an embassy to the Vatican. That huge open space, like the pool of a harbour between piers, is full of coaches, rumbling and lurching on their

springs, but glittering like chariots of crystal
and gold. Coachmen and postillions crack their
whips: heyducks and running footmen go before
the coaches, which tilt and fall upon the cobbles,
like sea-things going upon land, like the shells
of sea-borne Neptune come ashore. The horses
are urged into a gallop through the rainbow
spray; while the great piers of the colonnade
are crowded with statues, looking down on this
arrival. The procession comes to a halt and the
parti-coloured Swiss bring their halberds to
ground: and while the fountains still play their
colours on the wind, the Cardinal and his
retinue go up the Scala Regia of Bernini into
the court of the priest-king. This, for its mitres,
is a college of the priests of Isis, bringing the
temples of Old Nile out of the ancient history
of universal dominion. Such is the shadowy and
ghostly force of ancient Rome still living in the
only body that has survived its splendour.

This is the Piazza of St. Peter's, but there is,
as well, the Piazza Navona. It is to be seen in
pictures and engravings filled with figures, for
being one of the only wide spaces in Rome this

Rome

was where the crowds of Carnival spent their frenzy. We will look again at a picture by Pannini in order to hear them approaching. The rolling and tumbling of the Saltarello comes nearer and nearer, like a procession, gathering new actors at every street corner until it bursts into the square and takes possession of all that great area cooled with waters. The fountain of Bernini, with the four rivers of the world, Danube, Ganges, Nile and Plata, pouring from their urns, travesties, indeed, the four quarters of the globe, for the whole area of its beneficence jostles with masks, and this ancient circus of old Rome, this Stadium of Domitian, can have known no more noise where, so often, there had been the hush of excitement and the thrill of horror. The Piazza Navona, in the time of Carnival, was the vitality of Papal Rome, and to what was true of this festival in Venice, or elsewhere, was added the exuberance of the South. It was the focus of popular tunes, the paradise of the mandoline.

Here, a century later, during Carnival, there took place that curious episode when Paganini and Rossini, in disguise, played to the crowd; and the possibilities of this extraordinary popular festival were not exhausted until recent memory. In the early part of the eighteenth century we may suppose that the beauty of this scene of rejoicing was at its apogee, and, certainly the weedy tritons of the fountains and the great population of grotesque masks scattered by the Seicento wherever there was water, or even dry and empty-mouthed upon the walls at any angle where they could be seen, was an encouragement to the masquerade. The rest of the year, in Rome, it was penitence more than enjoyment that was encouraged, so that we may suppose the fullest opportunity was taken of this occasion.

Another point that must be considered in any account of the influence that residence in Rome is likely to have had upon a lively intelligence is the fact that it had, by then, become a part of the recognised education of every artist to be sent to Rome. Local notabilities in their encouragement of local talent, even in the most remotely bucolic parts of Europe, would combine together to send the neophyte to Rome. The Académie de France had been founded by Louis XIV as far back as 1666. Even before this Poussin and Claude had started the precedent; so that from the point of view of intelligent society its members were anything but exclusively Roman by birth. The proof of this is the meeting of Domenico Scarlatti and Handel. A new generation of painters arrived every few years to continue the endless discussions upon art; so that Rome was, at once, partly a university and partly the art school of the time in a sense in which its opinions could not be ignored, just as contemporary painters have to keep abreast of the movement in Paris. Rome was, also, the best possible centre of renown, for the news of personalities spread quickly from there into all the civilised quarters of Europe.

Doubtless it is for this reason that when Domenico Scarlatti next set out upon his travels, or, indeed, travelled for the first time anywhere out of Italy, it was to London that he went. This was in 1719; and he must have arrived in London in the midst of the tremendous operatic warfare between his friend Handel and Bononcini. The details of his stay in London are completely unknown to us, except that he renewed acquaintance with Handel, and that his opera *Narciso* was given on May 30, 1720; and as he stayed such a short time it is unnecessary to enlarge upon its possibilities, or its contingent results upon him. Another foreign tour that he undertook two years later is of far more importance, for it was to affect all the rest of his life.

V

Portugal

★

ꞁHE OBJECT OF THIS JOURNEY WAS LISBON,
and he arrived there during the reign of the
splendour-loving João V (1706-1750), perhaps
the most extravagant monarch who has ever
existed outside the history of the Orient. The
exploits of this extraordinary individual deserve
an enquiry as to his antecedents.

After the eighty years' captivity of Portugal
to Spain, her independence was at last achieved
and the monarchy restored in the person of the
Duke of Bragança, the head of an illegitimate
line descended from the original Kings. The
Duke of Bragança, who took the title of João IV,
was outside the usual inheritance of dynastic
blood into which the marriages of his descen-

dants were soon to plunge the Bragança family, for his mother was Donna de Velasco, daughter of the Duque de Frias, who was Constable of Castile. João IV was a musician of remarkable attainments. Music was the sole purpose of his life, and he was a very considerable composer. His wife was also of Spanish blood, being Donna Luisa Francisca de Guzman, daughter of the 8th Duke of Medina Sidonia. He had two sons, afterwards Alfonso VI and Pedro II: and João V, the subject of our enquiry, was son of the second of these, Pedro II, by Maria Sofia Isabel of Bavaria-Neuberg, a family with descent from the Medici.

João V had all the musical enthusiasm of his grandfather, without its creative side. And he was able to indulge these proclivities, and any other weaknesses that he possessed, to a degree that has scarcely a parallel in history. It was the discovery of gold in Brazil that allowed him credit for these multiple activities. The most famous of these was the palace of Mafra, which was designed to eclipse the Escurial. That is still standing, but nearly all his other buildings perished in the Lisbon earthquake of 1755; so that, in order to form an idea of his taste in luxury, it is necessary to seek out the collection of Germain silver and the Royal coaches at Belem. These are the minor things, the mere debris of his reign; but they provide the proofs of his astonishing cultivation of display. The Germain silver is in the National Museum at Lisbon. There are more than a thousand pieces of it, in gold and silver plate and enamel; dinner services, toilet sets, centre pieces for the table, and so forth; but, more especially, the famous breakfast service in gold by François Thomas Germain, the greatest of the French silversmiths, whose work hardly survives elsewhere. Other pieces are by Godin and by Cousinet. The Germain silver gives an idea of what must have been the fabulous luxury of the Court; but the sight of the Royal coaches at Belem confirms the wildest hazards.

The best of the coaches is the Coronation coach of João V, which is decorated with tortoiseshell, and those of the Marques de Fontes, which were used in his embassy to Pope Clement XI, in 1716. There are three of these; and they are just such as we have described in a previous paragraph, where we imagined their arrival beneath the colonnade of St. Peter's— except that we left out of account the gala-liveries of exotic pattern that will have been worn by the lacqueys. These three coaches have ivory fittings, curtains of gold brocade, and huge allegorical sculptures of Neptune and the sea-gods, in evocation of Portugal's past supremacy upon the ocean. Uniforms of indescribable magnificence were worn in these cavalcades, and as a public spectacle they must have been without parallel. Successive embassies were sent to Rome by João V, until, finally, his object was achieved and Benedict XIII made the Cardinal of Lisbon into a Patriarch, and allowed him to officiate in vestments resembling those of the Pope, and his canons in imitation of those of the cardinals. Finally, in the last year of his reign, the title of 'Fidelissimus', or 'Most Faithful', was conferred upon him, to correspond with those of 'Most Christian' and 'Most Catholic' attributed respectively to the Kings of France and Spain.

But the importance of this King to our narrative is in his love for music. He married Anna of Austria, daughter of the Emperor Leopold I, who, from her paternity, is certain to have been musical. It is, therefore, no matter for surprise that their daughter, the Infanta Barbara, who was to play so large a part in the life of Domenico Scarlatti, should have been not only a person of remarkable musical tastes, but, also, it would seem, the apt pupil of Scarlatti and a remarkable performer upon the harpsichord. Scarlatti had, in fact, arrived at Lisbon in order to be her music-master, but João had engaged the services of the foremost harpsichord of the day as teacher to all the Princesses, and the Infanta Barbara was so young, then, that she can only have shown the beginning of her talent.[1] It was only, as we shall see, at her marriage that she was able to give effect to

[1]The Infanta Barbara was born in 1711. At the date of Scarlatti's visit to Lisbon she was, therefore, only ten years of age.

her admiration of her music-master, and that he accepted permanent employment in her service.

Meanwhile, in parenthesis, it is tempting to the author to think that a magnificent red lacquer harpsichord and its stool, seen a few years ago in London by the writer of these pages, may conceivably have been played upon by Domenico Scarlatti. It was a present from João V to a nun, who was his mistress, and had only lately come out of the convent where she lived.[1] The date of this superb instrument, one of the finest works in red lacquer imaginable, was about 1720, so that, as it was the property of João V, it is not at all improbable that Scarlatti may have played upon it to the King during his visit to Lisbon.

In order to complete the picture of these musical activities, and to demonstrate, in doing so, the background of music out of which his patroness, the Infanta Barbara, was to emerge,

[1]Probably from the Cistercian convent at Odivelas, near Lisbon, which was the scene of João V's intrigue with Madre Paula, one of the nuns.

it must be stated that, later on in his reign, João V was to be the patron of Cafarelli and Egizziello, the greatest Castrati of the time. The opera, at Lisbon, was the best in Europe; and the palace choir, for which these singers were also engaged, was the finest body of singers of their day. The son of João, Dom José, who was brother to the Infanta Barbara, continued this lavish patronage of opera. In *Alessandro nell' Indie*, an opera by Perez, which was dedicated to Cafarelli, a whole troop of horses appeared on the stage, with a Macedonian phalanx. One of the King's riding-masters rode Bucephalus, to a march which Perez composed in the Manege, to the grand pas of a beautiful horse. As to the Royal Choir, it was still the most excellent in Europe so late as 1787, the year of Beckford's visit to Portugal, as we read in the following extract from his *Letters*. 'The Queen of Portugal's chapel is still the first in Europe, in point of vocal and instrumental excellence; no other establishment of the kind, the Papal not excepted, can boast such an assemblage of admirable musicians. Wherever her Majesty

Portugal

(Maria I)[1] moves they follow; when she goes a hawking to Salvaterra, or a health-hunting to the banks of the Caldas. Even in the midst of these wild rocks and mountains, she is surrounded by a bevy of delicate warblers, as plump as quails, and as gurgling and melodious as nightingales. The violins and violoncellos at her Majesty's beck are all of the first order, and in oboe and flute-players her musical menagerie is unrivalled. . . . This very morning, to my shame be it recorded, I remained hour after hour in my newly-arranged pavilion, without reading a word, writing a line, or entering into any conversation. All my faculties were absorbed by the harmony of the wind instruments, stationed at a distance in a thicket of orange and bay trees.'

During this early part of his reign, when Scarlatti visited Lisbon, the perfection of these musical arrangements had not yet been at-

[1]Maria I (1777-1816) was daughter of Dom José I, and married her father's brother, Dom Pedro III. He was brother, therefore, to the Infanta Barbara. After his death in 1786, the queen became insane. She was driven from Portugal to Brazil by the troops of Napoleon, and died at Rio de Janeiro.

[64]

tained, partly, it may be surmised, because the best singers were then engaged in London and were not available for Lisbon until the definite failure of Handel as an operatic composer. Once the scheme of establishing Italian opera on this scale in London had broken down, Lisbon became the centre of musical life, so far as this aspect of music was concerned.

The reverse of the picture is not so pleasant. The religious bigotry of João led to some appalling episodes, as witness the following letter, written to Bishop Burnet by Dr. Wilcox, afterwards Bishop of Gloucester, quoted in Chandler's *Limborch*, page 302, and dated Lisbon, Jan. 15, 1706. (This was in the first year of João's reign.)

'My Lord, in obedience to your Lordship's commands of the 12th I have sent all that was printed concerning the last auto-da-fé. I saw the whole process, which is agreeable to what was published by Limborch and others on the subject. Of the five persons condemned, there were but four burnt; Antonio Tavanes, by an unusual reprieve, being saved after the procession. Heytor Dias and Maria Penteyra were burnt alive, and the other two first strangled. The execution was very cruel. The woman was alive in the flames half an hour, and the man above an hour. The present King[1] and his two brothers were seated at a window so near as to be addressed to, a considerable time, in very moving terms, by the man as he was burning. But though the favour he begged was only a few more faggots, yet he was not able to obtain it. Those who are burnt alive here, are seated on a bench, twelve feet high, fastened to a pole, and about six feet higher than the faggots. The wind being a little fresh, the man's hinder parts were perfectly wasted; and as he turned himself, his ribs opened before he left speaking; the fire being recruited as it wasted, to keep him just in the same degree of heat. But all his entreaties could not procure him a larger allowance of wood to shorten his misery and despatch him. How hard must his heart be who can read this without horror!'

[1]The crime of having a nun for your mistress was apparently excused in the case of a King! Cf. p. 62.

Portugal

This shocking scene was repeated, at no infrequent intervals, throughout his reign; and some readers may be reminded of the even more appalling execution of the Tavora conspirators in 1760, under Dom José I. This was Portugal, but France was no better. The execution of Damien, under Louis XV, was no less terrible in its detail. Nor was the traitor's punishment meted out to the Jacobites after the '45 any less shameful as an indictment of its period.[1]

All these princes of the eighteenth century seem to our eyes like the survivors of some race of huge extinct animals sprawling upon the country. They are the dinosaurs of their day, fed upon a special diet. Europe was thick with them: whether we think of Louis XV and his Parc aux Cerfs: of Frederick the Great and his palaces and grenadiers: or of Augustus the Strong with his three hundred and sixty-five children. It was a race which, perhaps because

[1]Within the prison of York Castle there was to be seen, till recently, the gigantic knife and fork of iron with which the rebels were quartered.

it was so interrelated, is always true to type.
The pictures at Dresden, the fantastic skeleton
of the Zwinger, the porcelain of Meissen, the
Green Vaults with their unique works of the
goldsmith Dinglinger: these are the spiritual
assets of the gigantic Saxon. Also, he was a
devotee of music. But it is a type which can be
traced in innumerable examples through all the
German princelings; and its full examination
would yield us, as well, such figures as Gus-
tavus III of Sweden, with his theatre of Drott-
ningholm; King Stanislas, the patron of Héré
and Lamour at Nancy; Vittorio Amadeo II of
Savoy, the patron of Juvara; and, not least,
João V-of Portugal. This can be said for them,
that their fortunes were not expended on sub-
marines and poison-gas. For the most extravagant king is better than the cheapest war.

The typical princely patronage of the epoch
was shortly to be extended to Domenico Scarlatti in a manner which made him the exclusive
servant of his Royal mistress. In effect he was
withdrawn altogether from the public for the
space of a quarter of a century. He was to be the

private household artist of the King and Queen of Spain, and the conditions of his employment were of the same nature as those which secured the exclusive services of the goldsmith Dinglinger at Dresden, or those of the modellers Marcolini or Bustelli for the porcelain factories of Meissen and Nymphenburg. As a result of this Scarlatti's music was to remain almost entirely unknown to his contemporaries, except that part of it which he had completed prior to his departure from Italy.

Meanwhile, it is fascinating to contemplate the image of Scarlatti against the exotic background of Portugal. The age of João V was the second great period of Portuguese culture, comparable in many ways to the Manoeline age. João was a typical prince of the delayed Renaissance, and if it had not been for the earthquake of 1755, which destroyed Lisbon as Messina was destroyed, there would be more than sufficient evidence to establish the curious characteristics of this neglected period. The background is more than half oriental in nature, for this was the great epoch of polychrome tile-painting,

Portugal

and the entire walls of churches and of cloisters, the decoration of rooms, the panelling of staircases, even the façades of buildings, consisted entirely of those china landscapes and enamelled figures. The art of the azulejo is only to be appreciated in Portugal, and it is as typical of that country as marble is of Rome, or brick of Amsterdam.

vi

Naples Again

★

HE DOES NOT SEEM TO HAVE STAYED ANY LON-
ger in Lisbon than he did in London, but the
consequences of this visit were fraught with
life-long importance for him. Meanwhile, another eight years were to pass, which were spent
mainly at Naples, with journeys, it may be imagined, to other towns in Italy. These were the
years 1721 to 1729, the maturity of Scarlatti's
life, and a vast number of his harpsichord
sonatas must date from this period. In the next
phase of his life he was to be lost to the outside
world, so that the majority of his pieces that
were in circulation will have been the fruits of
this Neapolitan decade. The three hundred and
forty-nine pieces by Scarlatti in the collection

[71]

of the Abbé Santini, in contrast with the total edition of five hundred and forty-five sonatas in the definitive edition published in 1910, may give, in fact, the approximate total of his achievement up to his final removal from Naples to Spain. The characteristic atmosphere of Domenico Scarlatti is Neapolitan; and this has to be stressed in view of the fact that, by some curious aberration, if it is ever taken into account at all it is generally labelled as being typical of the Venetian eighteenth century, and is associated, for instance, with the pictures of Pietro Longhi. This mistaken attribution has been strengthened by the popularity of *The Good-Humoured Ladies*, the ballet contrived out of his music, which Diaghilev allowed to be transferred from Naples to Venice because Leon Bakst had always wished to attempt a setting in Venetian eighteenth-century style. Nothing could be farther from the truth; nor, it may be added, have the plays of Goldoni the slightest affinity to the music of Scarlatti. Their character is essentially different. Goldoni was typical of the middle and end of the century: he was the contemporary of Reynolds, Dr. Johnson, Garrick: Domenico Scarlatti, by contrast, lived in the time of Bach, Hogarth, Handel.

His music, while characteristic of a full and mature environment, is more alert and vigorous than any product of the contemporary Venetian mind. What Professor E. J. Dent has summed up as his 'neatly organised forms, his extraordinary modulations, his skill in thematic development, his quaint mannerism of reiterating character-istic figures', all these attributes are, surely, en-tirely urban in character. If the narrow streets of Naples are as crowded as the Venetian alleys, they have, at least, none of the impenetrable shadow of the canals, their water-born languor, their floating ease. Instead, they are alive with the noise of wheels and with the neighing of horses and mules. Venice was tumbling into decrepitude: she was lamenting her past gran-deur: not so, Naples, which, even then, was waiting to become a capital. It had not been the centre of a court for two centuries, although better suited to this purpose than any town in

Naples Again

Italy, and, at the date of which we are speaking, its importance as capital of a considerable kingdom lay still before it. No part of our present purpose would be served by expatiating on some forgotten aspects of the Bourbon rule, but under the Bourbons Naples was to have the first broad streets in Europe, the first streets lit by gas-lamps, and the first line of railway in Italy. From every point of view, in the first half of the eighteenth century, the greatness of Naples lay before her.

And, by the years of which we are treating, the musical life of Naples had still further developed. The elder Scarlatti died in 1725, but those other composers mentioned by Dr. Burney in his exordium of Naples were in their flower of achievement. We can do little more than recapitulate their names: Leonardo Leo, Pergolesi, Porpora, Farinelli, Jommelli, Traetta, Sacchini: to whom we may add Durante, Vinci, Logroscino. This list might be indefinitely extended; but, out of their whole total, it is only Domenico Scarlatti who has any contact with us over the centuries, and if any attempt is ever to be made to revive an interest in these dead men, it can be best attempted through an enlargement in our knowledge of their only survivor. It has, at least, been easy enough to place him in surroundings of the greatest possible energy and activity, where the force and variety of his talent are no longer difficult to explain.

The end of this epoch will have found Domenico Scarlatti in the full extension of his powers, both as composer and performer. It was an art of which he was the unique master. There can have been little direct competition, for Naples had no school, generally speaking, of composers for the harpsichord. But the greatest singers of all time, and, we may surmise, the greatest school of vocal writing, were in incessant productivity during these years. The great Porpora, who had opened his school of singing at Naples in 1712, had, by now, moved to Germany, where he was chamber-virtuoso to the Prince of Hesse-Darmstadt. Farinelli, Porporino, Cafarelli, Senesino, had been his pupils. But his place as composer was now occupied by the Saxon Hasse,[1] a pupil of the elder Scarlatti and a musician of supreme importance in his day, upon whose music it would be difficult for even the most learned theorist to pronounce a verdict, for it was destroyed almost in entirety during the siege of Dresden by Frederick the Great, in 1760. Hasse had collected nearly all his compositions at the request of Augustus III of Saxony, in order that they should be engraved and published, and the whole accumulation was set on fire and destroyed by the Prussian cannon. It is enough, without further details of such forgotten careers, to say that the virtuosity of this school of Neapolitan composers was not in the least improbable as background for such a virtuoso as Domenico Scarlatti. The terrifying nature of the ornamentation as practised by the Castrati in their singing made these quieter and more reasonable acrobatics of the keyboard into a display of comparative sobriety. It was virtuosity for the sake of virtuosity, but not ornament for the sake of ornament.

[1]Hasse heard Domenico Scarlatti play the harpsichord, at Naples, in 1725.

vii
A Double Wedding

★

IT WAS FROM THE MIDST OF THIS CEASELESS
ebullition that Scarlatti was, now, subtracted.
In effect, he was removed altogether from the
applause of the public, and was to devote the
rest of his life to the pleasures of an eccentric
court, who lived, of predilection, in the country
and hardly ever approached their own capital.
The offer must have been of a tempting character, financially, or it is not to be supposed that
the exile would have been accepted.

It was in 1729, when he was nearly forty-
five years of age, that Domenico Scarlatti set
sail for Spain to become virtuoso to the Princess
of the Asturias. For, in that same year, the
Prince of the Asturias, who was the eldest sur-

A Double Wedding

viving son of Felipe V of Spain, had been married to the Infanta Maria Magdalena Barbara of Bragança, daughter of João V of Portugal. The marriage had been made the excuse for unparalleled demonstrations of extravagance on the part of her father, culminating in the palace of Vendas Novas. This palace of fine stone, with its complete equipment of furniture and comforts, was built to accommodate the Court for one night only especially for this occasion. As there was no water near the palace, it was even brought at great expense from a fountain made for the purpose at Pegões, ten miles away, where, also João V built another Royal quinta.

In short, nothing was neglected. For it was to be a double marriage. Not only was the Prince of the Asturias to marry the Infanta Barbara, but his sister, the Infanta Maria Vittoria de Borbón, was to marry Dom José, the Heir-apparent to Portugal. As a result of this marriage a separate household had to be formed for the Prince of the Asturias, and the post of chamber-virtuoso was offered to Domenico Scarlatti and accepted by him.

A Double Wedding

Actually, his appointment was to the Infanta Barbara, so that it must have emanated from her side of the negotiations, and will have been the direct result of Scarlatti's visit to Lisbon, nearly ten years before. The reports of his prowess on the harpsichord will have been corroborated from Naples through the Portuguese Ambassador, or from members of one of the incessant missions that João V was always sending to the Pope, for these will have passed through Naples on their way to Rome. Music, as we have said, was in the blood of João V, and we shall soon see that it was not less strong in the veins of the Spanish Bourbons.

Felipe V, it will be remembered, was grandson to Louis XIV (being son of the Grand Dauphin and his wife Maria Anna of Bavaria). He was born at Versailles, and brought up at the court of Louis XIV under the title of Duc d'Anjou. In 1700, when the last Spanish Hapsburg, Carlos II died, Louis XIV promoted his grandson's succession to the throne and despatched him to Spain. The Wars of the Spanish Succession left him confirmed in his monarchy; while, as early as 1702, he had married Maria Luisa of Savoy. The children of this marriage were Luis I and Fernando VI. Felipe was profoundly melancholic, and in 1724 retired from the throne in favour of his son Luis I: but Luis died in seven months and Felipe again became King. The second son, Fernando, with whom we are concerned in these pages, then became Prince of the Asturias, and Heir to the Throne.

Meanwhile, by his second marriage to Elisabetta Farnese, Felipe had become father to four more sons; an eldest and imbecile child, set aside from the succession; the future Carlos III of Spain; the future Fernando IV of the Two Sicilies; and another son, Felipe, who inherited the Duchy of Parma through his mother Elisabetta Farnese, and was ancestor to the family of Bourbon-Parma. These are complicated details of the most intricate dynasty in history; but our only direct concern here is with Felipe V, the first Bourbon King of Spain, and with his eldest surviving son, the Prince of the Asturias, afterwards Fernando VI. Their wives were, respectively, Elisabetta Farnese, stepmother to Fernando, and the Infanta Barbara of Portugal. Domenico Scarlatti, as we have said, was attached to the household of the last-named Princess.

The Prince of the Asturias had been born in 1713. He was therefore, at the time of his marriage, only sixteen years of age. It is recorded that the Infanta Barbara's homely looks, on their first meeting, caused him a visible shock; but in the course of a very few years he had become devoted to her. Their first sight of each other will have taken place, in all probability, at that palace of Vendas Novas that we have just described. The building, mostly one-storeyed, with a part of its neglected gardens, is still standing in our day, but has been turned into a cavalry-barracks. But, for nearly two centuries, this palace of Vendas Novas was locked up and uninhabited,[1] waiting for the Court to arrive

[1]Beckford slept a night in the palace of Vendas Novas, on his way from Portugal to Spain, in November 1787. A young priest was the solitary inhabitant, and Beckford notices its extensive façade, and the painted ceilings of the rooms. He also comments upon the solidity of the building and its excellent state of preservation after being empty for so long.

again with its train of halberdiers and negro pages, with its fantastically garbed dwarfs, and its rhapsodists sporting impromptu verses as though in the worst throes of echolalia.

This is the Court of Portugal as echoed by Beckford in his *Letters*. He describes retinues of this sort, as seen by him, in the decaying years of this extravagance, nearly forty years after the death of João V, when Portugal had been ruined by the earthquakes of Lisbon. But, on the occasion of this double marriage, the scene will have been still more extraordinary, complicated by the presence of the Spanish Court, as well. The collection of dynastic faces will have been a sight in itself. For the descendants of Charles V and of Louis XIV, interrelated by inextricable ramifications, were a race by themselves. Their coincidence in such quantity in these strange surroundings raises the whole episode of this double-marriage of Vendas Novas into the improbability of a fairy-tale. It is the Lac des Cygnes or La Belle au bois dormant realised in actual fact and historically proved. Certainly no more curious gathering than those who spent this one night under that roof can be imagined; and its fantastic unreality is increased by the early ages of the contracting parties. They were mere children.

The Infanta Maria Vittoria, who was to marry Dom José de Portugal, was the eldest daughter of Felipe V by his second marriage to Elisabetta Farnese. She was only fourteen years of age. The Prince of the Asturias, her half-brother, was sixteen years old. Carlos III, who was successively Duke of Parma, King of Naples, and King of Spain, was her full-brother. His age was eleven. It is an illustration of the incredible circumstances in which their lives were conducted that Carlos III and his sister did not meet again, from 1729 until 1777, a space of forty-eight years. She returned to Spain after the death of her husband, José I of Portugal, and Carlos came out a long journey to meet her, for the brother and sister were extremely devoted to each other; but even the most loyal and affectionate among the courtiers, so we are told by contemporary writers, could hardly restrain their amusement at the sight of this aquiline and untidy old Infanta shooting from horseback with her brother, and appearing unmoved by the most strenuous exertion.

Such long separations were common in dynastic families, for the same situation, only with an unsatisfactory solution, was repeated in the next generation, in the children of Carlos III. He had withdrawn from Naples, in 1759, to become King of Spain, leaving his third son, Ferdinando, a boy of eight, as King of Naples, and taking back with him his second son, Carlos IV of Spain, who is familiar to us in the portraits of Goya. In the course of time Carlos IV was exiled from his kingdom, owing to the Napoleonic Wars,-and the two brothers had no opportunity of meeting from 1759 until 1817, an interval of fifty-eight years, when the dying wish of the King of Spain to see his brother could not cut short the King of Naples' day of shooting.

The assembly at Vendas Novas for this pair of child marriages was the prelude to an immense journey home through wooded Estremadura and the high Castilian plain. It will have occupied at least two weeks. The Prince and Princess of the Asturias will have ridden on mules or been carried in litters, and must have slept for most of the journey in tents. The largest caravan of the desert cannot have exceeded in the number of retinue and the train of baggage animals. They must have eaten up the lean countryside. Provisions had been left behind, we may suppose, on their outward journey to Portugal, but, during their absence, flocks of geese had been driven in from the farms, lambs had been slaughtered, and every preparation made for the return of this small army. It is tempting to think of their progress through Estremadura, among the oak woods and the herds of swine, into the high heart of Spain and the burnt Castilian colours, but there is no space for that.

viii

Spain

★

DOMENICO SCARLATTI ARRIVED TO TAKE UP
his service to the Infanta Barbara in the very
year of her marriage. The Prince of the Asturias
seems to have had no official duties whatever to
fulfil. The actual government of Spain was in
the more than capable hands of his stepmother, Elisabetta Farnese. His father, Felipe V,
left everything entirely to her devices, and she
ruled the country and intervened decisively in
its foreign policies. The Prince and Princess of
the Asturias lived in apartments in the same
palace as the King and Queen. They had their
own establishment, but no palace of their own.
Felipe V had a horror of the Escurial, and tried
to limit his visits to the minimum of his official

duties. He will have heard only too many details, long before he reached Spain, of the Pudridero, the vault of his ancestors. A macabre horror attaches to every circumstance known of his predecessor, Carlos II, the last of the Spanish Hapsburgs. This feudal, or heraldic ghost, nearly incapable of speech and quite impossible of procreation, was fed at the breast till nearly twenty years of age, while his amusements were divided between catching butterflies with buttered cabbage-leaves, and haunting the Pudridero, where, on occasion, he would have a coffin opened that he might gaze upon his ancestors and compare their mouldering features with his own long chin and flaxen hair, the birthright of his race. He was surrounded in all his actions by an inflexible and rigid etiquette, of Pharaonic formality, so that the contemplation of his life of forty years is one of the curiosities of history. Eventually, and long after it was overdue, he, too, reposed in the Pudridero; and it is understandable that his French successor, Felipe V, dreaded, above all else, eventual burial in that ghastly charnel house. We shall see that he and his son were the only Spanish monarchs who ever avoided this commitment to their grisly ancestors. Father and son were exactly alike in this; and, indeed, in everything that is known of their characters. But it would be no exaggeration to say that the strongest trait that they had in common was their love for music. The evidence as to this mutual proclivity is overwhelming.

But, having embarked Scarlatti for Spain, it is necessary to define the locality. His official duties can hardly have taken him to more than three places, Madrid, Aranjuez and La Granja. Felipe V scarcely ever visited the South, for even the comparative luxury of Seville was distasteful to him. His favourite residence was La Granja, and, to a lesser degree, Aranjuez. The latter place is about thirty miles from Madrid, and is so completely changed in character owing to alterations and additions made in the style and period of the Empire that it hardly repays examination. In any case, only a portion of it was finished by Felipe V, and the remainder is the work of Carlos III and Carlos IV, both of whom are outside the scope of these pages.

But La Granja still retains a great deal of the character that it must have possessed under Felipe V and Fernando VI. Felipe, who was born at Versailles and had a Frenchman's nostalgia for France, wanted to build a palace and garden in the French taste in some spot, sufficiently remote, and yet not too far from the capital. He found the site while hunting near Segovia in the year 1720, and bought it from the monks of El Parral. The very next year work was begun, and by 1723 Felipe was in residence. The palace was built by Theodore Artemans to the designs of the Sicilian architect Juvara, a neglected genius, who worked most of his life in Turin for Vittorio Amadeo II of Savoy. He was one of the very first artists of the Baroque age, and, in addition, a magnificent designer for the theatre, not inferior, in fact, to Ferdinando Bibiena.

The gardens and fountains, which are the glory of La Granja, were begun in 1727 at the instigation of Elisabetta Farnese. There are no fewer than twenty-six monumental fountains, chiefly by Frémin and Thierri, and they are even superior to those at Versailles. The chief of them is los baños de Diana, with the goddess coming out of the water in the midst of a band of twenty naked nymphs; while another, the fountain of Fame, throws a jet of water one hundred and thirty feet into the air. The actual gardens were laid out to the designs of René Carlier and Boutelou, but their whole site of three hundred and fifty acres is so vast that it took no less than three generations of French sculptors and gardeners to complete the scheme. It was not finished until late in the reign of Carlos III. The interior of the palace, which had magnificent furniture, was destroyed by a disastrous fire in 1918, and is no longer worth seeing. But the Colegiata, built in the form of a Latin cross, with a fine marble altar designed by Solimena at Naples, contains the tombs of Felipe and Elisabetta Farnese, who contrived successfully to escape the Escurial.

This palace of La Granja and its gardens were, in fact, tolerably complete by 1729. They have not been much altered since the Prince of the Asturias and his wife took up residence, with Scarlatti in their suite. It is still a place of extraordinary beauty, even if the fountains are not playing, an exception which is only contradicted for three days in the year. Then, the sight is of unimaginable loveliness; while the thought of the strange inhabitants who, long ago, passed the summers in this rarefied air lends an added beauty to the music of the waters.

All to do with La Granja is artifice: beginning with the aerial improbability of its situation, for while upon the same latitude as Naples, its elevation, of all but four thousand feet above the sea, is higher than the crater of Vesuvius. Nearly all the year round there is snow only a few minutes' walk up the mountain side. No place could be more lovely for the heats of summer than La Granja; and in winter, coming back from hunting in the woods, the crackle of the fire must have seemed more grateful for the frost outside. And, as we shall see, the recreation of those hours not spent in the chase was centred in music.

Spain

After La Granja, the palaces at Madrid remain to be described. In this year, 1729, which
marked the arrival in the capital of our hero
and of the newly-wedded Prince and Princess of
the Asturias, the old Royal Palace was still
standing. It was burnt down on Christmas Eve,
1734, and many masterpieces of painting must
have perished in the flames. Pictures by Roger
van der Weyden, Hieronymus Bosch, Titian,
Rubens and Velasquez are known to have been
destroyed. Felipe, thereupon, sent for Juvara
from Turin, who prepared a model, which is
still in existence, for a palace 1700 feet square,
100 feet high, with a courtyard 700 by 400 feet.
But Juvara died in Madrid, the next year, before
the plans could be proceeded with, having re-
commended his pupil Sacchetti to Felipe as the
best architect alive. A much smaller plan was
suggested by Sacchetti, and the existing Royal
Palace, of giant dimensions, was begun. It is an
adaptation of Bernini's rejected design for the
Louvre, although this interesting fact does not
seem to be generally known. Work on the
palace proceeded all through the reigns of

Spain

Felipe V and Fernando VI, while it was left to Carlos III to complete its decoration with the superb frescoes of Tiepolo in the Throne Room.

William Beckford, who visited the Palace in 1787, gives us an interesting sketch of its interior. The King (it was then Carlos III) was away on one of his eternal shooting expeditions, but Beckford so well describes the palace atmosphere that the absence is not noticed. In every room he passed through stood cages of gilded wire, and in every cage a curious exotic bird in full song. Mingling with these warblings were heard at certain intervals the low chimes of musical clocks, stealing upon the ear like the low tones of harmonic glasses. No other sound broke in upon the stillness except, indeed, the almost inaudible footsteps of several aged domestics, in court dresses of the cut and fashion prevalent in the days of the King's mother, Elizabeth Farnese, gliding along cautiously and quietly to open the cages and offer their inmates dainties such as highly educated birds should relish. While seeing over the rooms of this palace he enquired after a remarkable room called the 'Salón de los Funciones' or 'El Coliseo'. The ceiling had been painted by Raphael Mengs, and was one of his chief works: here Ferdinand and Barbara, the most musical of sovereigns, used to melt in ecstasies at the soft warblings of Farinelli and Egizziello.[1] Alas! for Beckford's pleasure. Not later than the previous summer this grand theatrical apartment had been divided into a suite of shabby, bandboxical rooms, for the accommodation of Dom Ferdinando, the Infant of Parma. No mercy had been shown to the beautiful roof. In some places legs and folds of drapery were still visible, but workmen and stuccadors were working at a

[1]There is a mistake here. Mengs was only called to Spain by Carlos III in 1761, two years after the death of Fernando VI. After some months, in the eloquent words of Fuseli's *Dictionary of Painters*, 'excess of application, and some disgusts, which too often are excited by envy of distinguished merit, threw him into a state of marasmus,' and he returned to Rome. He came back to Spain in 1773. Mengs, therefore, cannot have painted this ceiling. It seems more probable that it was by Corrado Giaquinto (1699-1765), a Neapolitan painter. Also, to the best of my belief, the room in question was at Aranjuez and not at Madrid.

Spain

great rate, and in a few days whitewash would
cover all this former glory.

Beckford's description of the palace can still
be verified in at least one of its rooms. This is
the Salón de Gasparini, decorated by the artist
of that name with woven hangings in silk, of an
indescribable richness. The room still contains
an immense number of musical clocks, many of
which date from the reign of Fernando and
Barbara. But the amateur must be warned that
the china of Buen Retiro and Capodimonte
dates, without exception, from the reign of
Carlos III. If we want the relics of Fernando
and Barbara, it is necessary to be content with
the musical clocks.

Another palace that must have been known
to Scarlatti is that of Buen Retiro. This was in
a suburb of Madrid, and its chief interest is that
when it was burnt down, in 1734, many of the
finest pictures of Titian were destroyed in the
flames, and it is estimated that at least one-third
of the entire output of Velasquez perished
on this occasion. The palace contained a very
large number of his finest paintings, which

are not even preserved to us in engravings, being part of the private royal collections and inaccessible to strangers. Buen Retiro has, also, a theatrical history, for when it was originally built in 1630 for Felipe IV by the Conde Duque de Olivares (the subject of a magnificent portrait by Velasquez), a theatre was attached in which the plays of Lope de Vega were first acted.

After the fire the palace remained in ruins, but was rebuilt with a new theatre, by Fernando VI. The following description is quoted from *A Journey through Spain in the years* 1786 *and* 1787, by Joseph Townshend. 'The palace of Buen Retiro is a vast pile of buildings long deserted, and, when I saw it, verging to decay. The theatre is vast and opens into the gardens so as to make them, upon occasion, a continuation of the scene. Here Fernando VI frequently amused the public with operas, of which his Queen Barbara of Portugal was extravagantly fond. The great saloon, called "El Cason", with its ceiling painted by Luca Giordano, remains a monument of his taste, invention, judgment, and imitative powers.[1] In the principal apartment of the roof is represented Hercules giving the Golden Fleece to Philip the Good, Duke of Burgundy. In a subordinate compartment Pallas and the Gods are seen subduing the Titans, answering to which the Majesty of Spain appears ruling the terrestrial globe. The rest is filled up with allegorical figures, finely expressed. The antechamber contains the Conquest of Granada. From the great saloon we go to the garden by a little oval cabinet, covered entirely with looking-glass, in the ceiling of which is represented the Birth of the Sun, with people of all nations worshipping the rising deity, whilst the priests are engaged in offering sacrifices. This, likewise, is by Giordano.'

These accounts by Beckford and by Townshend all lay stress, it will be noticed, upon the

[1]This hall, which is still in existence as the Museo de Reproducciones Artisticas, is a relic from the old Buen Retiro, having survived the fire. It was frescoed by Luca Giordano to the order of Carlos II. Giordano was in Spain from 1692 till 1700. But the antechamber and the oval cabinet described by Townshend are no longer in existence.

musical tastes of Fernando and Barbara. 'The warblings of Farinelli and Egizziello' were to sound through these various palaces only a few years after the arrival of Scarlatti in Spain. But, indeed, the whole episode of Farinelli reads like a fairy story.

This greatest of the Castrati, and probably the most skilled and beautiful singer who has ever lived, was called to Spain by Elisabetta Farnese in 1736 in order to cure her husband's melancholy. It will be remembered that Felipe had already resigned the throne in 1724 from melancholia, only to resume it again, seven months later, on the death of his son Luis I. The effect of Farinelli's singing upon Felipe was in the nature of a miraculous cure, but it had to be continued daily. He soothed Felipe's disordered mind every night for ten years with the same four songs, which he must have repeated altogether some three thousand six hundred times. He acted as unofficial Prime Minister, was given a salary of fifty thousand francs, and was made a Knight of Calatrava, one of the highest orders of Spanish chivalry. He was bound by strict contract to sing for the King and for no one else. One day, so we are informed, Elisabetta Farnese even kept him to his contract by a refusal to allow the Prince of the Asturias and his wife to hear him sing.

But the most curious point is that, on the death of Felipe V in 1746, Farinelli remained in office and performed exactly the same services for the Prince of the Asturias, now become Fernando VI. In fact, he was an even more fervent patron of Farinelli than his father, increasing the Castrati's allowances, and letting his influence in politics increase rather than diminish. The same four songs were sung to him nightly, his favourite being 'Son qual nave' from the opera *Eumene*, by Porpora, of whom Farinelli was the pupil. For twenty years, and more, Farinelli remained in royal favour with the two Kings. A quarter of a century had passed since the tumult of his youth, when he sang in London and his success in Porpora's operas caused Handel to leave the operatic stage and concentrate on oratorio. During all this time he had been, in effect, lost to the world: his continuance in favour was only to expire with the King. At the death of Fernando VI, in 1759, he was pensioned off by Carlos III and retired to Bologna, where he lived in luxury till 1782 and was visited by Dr. Burney, who leaves a fascinating account of their interview.

Egizziello, the other Castrati mentioned by Beckford, has a name which wonderfully suggests in its sound the warbling and trilling of some exotic bird. It is a disillusionment to learn that he was called Egizziello from his master, Domenico Gizzi. After Farinelli, he was the greatest of the Castrati. In 1742 he sang in Lisbon for João V, and two years later was engaged by Ferdinand and Barbara to sing at Madrid in the *Achille in Sciro* of Pergolesi. Another great singer, Cafarelli, had to come all the way from Poland in order to appear in this opera at Madrid. Cafarelli was the most grotesque of all the Castrati, having the personality of the true eunuch, so that he appears more like a character from a Turkish fairy story, or even from the *Arabian Nights*, than a live person historically proved, who was famous all over civilised

Europe only two centuries ago. He had been the pupil of Porpora, who kept him on one vocal exercise alone for five or six years until he had acquired perfection. Cafarelli, as well as Egizziello, was employed at Lisbon by João V, the father of the Infanta Barbara. At the age of sixty-five Cafarelli was still singing, and had bought the Neapolitan Dukedom of San Dorato, where he lived in great splendour. He died in 1783, leaving his great fortune and the dukedom to a nephew.

These details of the Castrati are given here because they are fascinating in themselves, and for the importance that they possess as evidence of the musical proclivities of Felipe V and his son Fernando VI. Their wives, Elisabetta Farnese and the Infanta Barbara, possessed these tastes to just as high a degree. The two Kings, indeed, were interchangeable as characters; but not the Queens.

Elisabetta Farnese was a woman of lively intelligence with the mind of a conspirator. Her instrument was Cardinal Alberoni; and her objects were to secure the kingdom of Naples and the Duchy of Parma as appanages for her sons. Her stepchildren were already provided for in Spain, but she wished to secure an inheritance for her own children.[1] The future Carlos III of Spain was sent at an early age to Parma, and thence to Naples, where he became King. He was succeeded at Parma, of which she was heiress, by the Infante Felipe, her second son; so that, to this extent, her plans were an unqualified success, and the division of the unwieldy Spanish monarchy into two halves, Spain and Naples, following the earlier precedent of the Emperor Charles V, was part of her scheme to secure thrones for her sons.

The Infanta Barbara, on the other hand, seems to have possessed intelligence for music alone, and it is even hinted that she may have been less than half-witted at anything else. Her passion was for music, and where she is ever mentioned in conjunction with her master Scarlatti,

[1]The Farnese family were famed for two things, fatness, and fertility. The latter of these traits is exemplified, even now, in the family of Bourbon-Parma. The present Duke of Parma is one of eighteen children, while his sister, the Empress Zita, has no less than eight.

it is on the assumption that as a performer she was the most promising of his pupils.[1] In appearance, she was of the dwarf Bragança type, very swarthy and thick-lipped, through her descent from the Emperor Leopold I.

This monarch, it may be noted, had an almost exact counterpart in our own Charles II, who inherited his characteristic swarthiness through Hapsburg descent. Leopold I, as we have already stated, was a musician of marked attainments, and it was the conjunction of his blood with that of the composer-King, João IV, which produced the Infanta Barbara. If we want to know her appearance we need only see a portrait of Catherine of Bragança, who was her great-aunt. In the court-dress of Velasquez, as still worn in her day by Queens and Infantas of Spain, the Infanta Barbara must have presented the most curious sight.

The extraordinary lengths to which over-

[1]She had a harpsichord which went up to G (as proved by Scarlatti's pieces written specially for her). Mr. J. B. Trend was recently given special facilities to search the Spanish Royal Palaces for this instrument, but he was unable to locate it.

breeding had gone in the production of heredi-
tary rulers is exemplified, as nowhere else, in
the persons of Fernando and Barbara. Music
was the solace of this strange pair. Their patronage of Farinelli, of Egizziello, of Cafarelli,
must be set beside their employment of Domenico Scarlatti. But the twenty-five years spent
by this musician in Spain are the most mysterious part of his whole career. It is nearly impossible to discover any details at all about his employment. His situation was, in all probability,
that of a superior servant; and, almost certainly,
he will have had to wear the livery of his
master. But the reason for this strange silence
about him is not difficult to seek. In Naples, he
was in the midst of a society of professional
musicians: his works were collected and com-
mented upon. But at Madrid, and more especially at Aranjuez and La Granja, he was quite
outside the communication of learned society.
The King, and the Prince and Princess of the
Asturias, were ill with melancholia, and were
uneducated in everything but their love of
music. They had no friends, and cared for the

society of none but themselves. It was only Elisabetta Farnese who maintained contact with the outside world. When her husband died, in 1746, and she withdrew in solitude to the palace of Rio Frio in the woods of Segovia, Fernando and Barbara were left alone except for their personal attendants. Elisabetta, it must be remembered, was only stepmother to Fernando; and, by this time, her sons were in secure possession of Parma and The Two Sicilies. When she died, in 1766, her lifework was accomplished.

She had, in fact, outlived Fernando and Barbara. And the mention of this tempts us to bring their lives, also, to a conclusion, so as to leave us free of dates. Fernando and Barbara, who had their parent's horror of the Escurial, determined to be buried in some church of their own choice. The Infanta Barbara built for this purpose, at her own expense, the enormous nunnery of Las Saleses Reales, in Madrid. It is a second Escurial, for size, and was designed in imitation of Madame de Maintenon's St. Cyr, as a place of retreat for herself when she became a widow. Actually, she died a year before her husband, who was distracted with grief and would not even dress, but wandered, unshaven and unwashed, in a nightgown, about the park of La Granja. He refused solace, even from the songs of Farinelli, and died the next year, even before their tomb in Las Saleses Reales was ready for them. They had reigned from 1746 to 1759, and were childless. Their death was the signal for the return of Farinelli to Italy, in receipt of a large pension from the new King, Carlos III, who came from Naples to take up the Spanish throne.

Several years before this, in 1754, Scarlatti had gone back to Naples, but we will delay this point in order to discuss his residence in Spain in the light of all the available information upon him. And, as we shall see, there is a certain amount of evidence to be found as to his activities outside that land, during this long exile of a quarter of a century.

ix

A Visit to Dublin

★

ALL THE KNOWN DETAILS CONCERNING SCAR-
latti, outside Spain, during this period, are connected with one episode alone, his visit to his
English friend, Thomas Roseingrave. On his return from Rome to England Roseingrave had
been made organist at St. George's, Hanover
Square. This was in 1725. Soon afterwards
tragedy descended upon him; and the details
are so curious that it is worth while to quote
them from Dr. Burney. 'Roseingrave having a
few years after this election fixed his affections
on a lady of no dove-like constancy, was rejected by her at the time he thought himself
most secure of being united to her for ever. This
disappointment was so severely felt by the un-

[109]

fortunate lover as to occasion a temporary and whimsical insanity. He used to say that the lady's cruelty had so literally and completely broke his heart, that he heard the strings of it crack at the time he received his sentence; and, on that account, ever after called the disorder of his intellect his crepation, from the Italian verb crepare, to crack. After this misfortune, poor Roseingrave was never able to bear any kind of noise without great emotion. If, during his performance of the organ at church, anyone near him coughed, sneezed or blew his nose with great violence, he would instantly quit the instrument and run out of church, seemingly, in the greatest pain and terror, crying out that it was Old Scratch who tormented him and played on his crepation.'

In the end Roseingrave was forced to resign his post at St. George's, and he retired to Dublin. It was there that Domenico Scarlatti visited him, in 1740. Another eye-witness, Archdeacon Cox, tells us that 'he was perfectly rational upon every subject but the one nearest his heart; whenever that was mentioned he was quite insane'. He still played superbly upon the harpsichord, especially extempore, and was well enough, not only to write music himself, but to edit, after Scarlatti's death, his friend's 42 *Suites of Lessons* published by John Johnson, at the Harp and Crown, Cheapside. Roseingrave was blamed in his lifetime for crude harmony and extravagant modulation, epithets sufficient in themselves to draw interest to him from a modern audience.[1]

It must have been a strong degree of personal affection for his old friend that drew Scarlatti all the way from Madrid to Dublin in order to see him. This was in the autumn of 1740; and all else that is known of this visit is that Scarlatti must have stopped in London on his way back, as is proved by the songs that he contributed to two pasticcio operas, *Alessandro in Persia* and *Merope*, produced in London in the spring of 1741. This journey to England is shrouded in

[1]Serge de Diaghilev, who was introduced to Roseingrave's music by Mr. Constant Lambert, had the intention of producing some of his works as a ballet, but his own death intervened.

mystery, though it may be thought certain that Scarlatti will have taken the opportunity to visit Handel. The complete silence regarding this episode is more peculiar because Dublin was, at that time, far from being as remote as it is now. It was the third city in Europe, in point of popularity, while the fact that Handel first produced *The Messiah* in Dublin is proof that it was something of a musical centre. This only serves to deepen the mysterious silence regarding Scarlatti's visit to these islands. It would be imagined that much excitement and controversy would have been aroused by his reappearance in England, but if this was the case no traces of it have survived. In short, nothing whatever is known of his visit to London and Dublin.

X

The Spanish Idiom in Scarlatti's Music

★

NOW, TO REVERT TO SPAIN, OUR ENDEAVOUR throughout these pages has been to show that Domenico Scarlatti was a conspicuous member of a society that was most acutely aware of its own environment. The school of Naples produced such men as Salvator Rosa, who was musician as well as painter, and Ferdinando Sanfelice, who was poet as well as architect. The arts, at Naples, were not divorced from each other. Music was such a common part of life at Naples that no one was ignorant of its charms. Equally, in that hive of energy and gesture, the musicians knew the writers and painters. Besides this, Scarlatti had lived for ten years in

The Spanish Idiom in Scarlatti's Music

Rome, which was the capital of the arts. It is, therefore, only reasonable to assume that he had eyes for his environment.

This could be proved definitely and beyond any doubt if it were possible to separate the sonatas written by him in Naples or Rome from those composed by him during his twenty-five years' residence in Spain. But it is a task which can only be accomplished by minute technical research. All that can be attempted in these unprofessional pages is an illumination of his background. Once it is established that he was in the service of two of the most sensitive, if eccentric, music-lovers that can be imagined, and that artists of the calibre of a Farinelli and an Egizziello were his daily companions, it should be more easy to complete the picture of his activities as portrayed in his music.

The chief interest of such an examination would be the proof it would afford of the extent to which Scarlatti allowed himself to be influenced by Spanish music. For the Spanish idiom, as known to us in Bizet, Chabrier, Debussy, Albeniz, is present in Domenico Scarlatti. This

The Spanish Idiom in Scarlatti's Music
was well known to Dr. Burney. In his words:
'There are many passages in Scarlatti's pieces,
in which he imitated the melody of tunes sung
by carriers, muleteers, and common people'.
This is pointed out again in Mr. J. B. Trend's
book on Manuel de Falla. 'Another interesting
feature of Domenico Scarlatti's harmonic style
is his fondness for internal pedal notes, often
leading to most surprising dissonances, which
many editors of the last century discreetly ex-
punged. Such passages are probably the result
of Scarlatti's acquaintance with the Spanish
guitar. The harpsichord can suggest vividly
the twanging effects of the guitar, and these
sounds were probably as stimulating to Scarlatti as was the ripple of the modern piano to
Chopin.'[1]

After Scarlatti, the Spanish idiom does not
appear in music for nearly a century, until its
faint echoes come again in the overture to

[1] The invaluable Dr. Burney tells us that he was
shown several Spanish harpsichords by Farinelli, in his
retirement at Bologna. The natural keys were black, the
flats and sharps covered with mother-of-pearl, and the
case of the instrument of cedar-wood.

The Spanish Idiom in Scarlatti's Music
Preciosa, a gypsy opera by Weber, and in the
Summer Night in Madrid of Glinka. Unless, indeed, it is true that there are traces of this influence in some of the music of another Italian
who lived in Spain, Boccherini. This unfortunate Venetian, who crowned a life of poverty by
dying virtually of starvation, had spent up-
wards of forty years in Madrid. M. Georges de
Saint-Foix, the great authority on Mozart, on
presenting his revised edition, in 1930, of an
old book on Boccherini by A. Picquot, published in 1851, gives instances in which he
claims to have discovered definite traces of the
popular Spanish music in some of Boccherini's
compositions. More especially in the music of a
ballet which is preserved, unpublished, in the
Library at Stuttgart, and which the learned
author states to be founded entirely on Spanish
dance rhythms. If this is so, it is one of the
earliest examples known of the adoption of
characteristic national rhythms by a serious
composer. Boccherini, the composer of one hundred and two string-quartets and one hundred
and twenty quintets, has sunk into such neglect

that it would be no more than a work of charity to rescue some of his compositions from the oblivion into which they have fallen. Sir Thomas Beecham has performed a symphony by Boccherini, but this is only a beginning. I should like to suggest, however, that a musician of the sensibility and education of Boccherini may well have possessed himself of some of the manuscripts of Scarlatti, his predecessor by only fifteen years of arrival in Spain.

Domenico Scarlatti may be credited, then, with the anticipation of effects only emulated by other composers nearly a century after his death. And that later division of his sonatas that comprises those written under, so to speak, the Spanish influence, gains in interest because of their haphazard occurrence in the complete edition. If they were collected together and presented as a definite body of his work, the general verdict upon Scarlatti would have to undergo a complete revision in the light of this new evidence. They are convincing proofs of his extreme originality, sounding curious enough to us, now, but in their time without precedent.

The Spanish Idiom in Scarlatti's Music

This accession of new material should make a drastic change in our opinion of Scarlatti. He has for too long been regarded as the most obligingly quaint of the old masters: a composer whose works can be opened on any page, at random, without the danger of dullness or disappointment. At the same time, curiosity has not led even the most eclectic of musicians to include more than the three or four most hackneyed of his works in their repertory. Anything like a considered group of his compositions seems never to appear in any programme. If this is of instinct, because his music sounds to better advantage in the home than in the concert-hall, there is reason and intelligence behind this accusation of ignorance. And yet, unless Scarlatti emerges into full light before the public, he can never fill the shadows. It is important, therefore, that he should be arraigned in the illumination of all the evidence that is available.

Let us repeat, for this purpose, that sentence from the preceding page: 'The harpsichord can suggest vividly the twanging effects of the guitar, and these sounds were probably as stimulating to Scarlatti as was the ripple of the modern piano to Chopin.' It would appear that there has always been a body of serious composers for the guitar in Spain. This fact will become plain to anyone who has ever heard Señor Segovia play pieces by Sor, Torroba, or Tarrega. They are conclusive evidence as to that. Now, no musician of the standing of Domenico Scarlatti could live for more than a few days in Madrid without meeting all the contemporary talent,[1] so that it is probable that his inspiration came alike from the professional players of that instrument, the sort of persons who would be employed in giving lessons to the young Spanish ladies, and, also, from the street-musicians. As for these latter, the most vital of the music was, of course, theirs; and it is interesting to re-

[1]A forgotten composer, Francisco Soler (d. 1783), was a pupil of Scarlatti. He wrote harpsichord pieces and chamber music. Soler was a monk at the Escurial. Some of his music has lately been published in Spain, and there is a revival of interest in him. Twenty-seven of his sonatas were published in London, by Robert Birchall, about 1790.

The Spanish Idiom in Scarlatti's Music
call that, a century and a half before this, almost the only item that has come down to us of personal information about the life of El Greco in Toledo tells us of his extravagance in hiring musicians to play to him, and of his delight in music. This will have been music of the street, probably of the Flamenco character, for there was none other except in the churches. Toledo was still a bilingual city of Arabic and Spanish in El Greco's day, and the music will have been less sophisticated than in the time of Scarlatti. But, even so, its peculiar flavour will have been quite unspoilt in the 'thirties and 'forties of the eighteenth century. The accounts of the fandango in Casanova's *Memoirs* and in the *Letters* of Beckford are evidence of the lively character and fire of the dance. Its slower and sadder measures will have been more likely to influence a musician, and there are certainly instances of this in some of Scarlatti's music at this period.

The background to the popular life of that time is to be found in Goya's tapestries, which are intended as scenes from popular life. They

The Spanish Idiom in Scarlatti's Music
are fifty years later in date, but Spain is a
country that changes so slowly that they are
true of the middle of that century just as much
as of its closing years. Also, the aim of Goya in
these cartoons was to present the typical and
traditional Spain of the lower orders. The
latest fashions in dress were no part of his plan,
so that the costumes worn in the tapestries are
approximately the dresses that will have been
worn by the peasants and middle-classes under
Felipe V and Fernando VI. It may be said with
truth that these scenes, also, 'suggest vividly the
twanging effects of the guitar'. Certain of them
could not be improved upon as illustrations for
that purpose. Indeed, we may parallel the fore-
going quotation by saying that those sounds
were as stimulating to Goya as was the ripple
of the modern piano to Chopin.

Such was Spain, and it is fascinating to seek
for it in Scarlatti. It comes in snatches like the
singing of the muleteers. Sometimes the strum-
ming is but an idle prelude that leads into a
classical portico and progresses in Italian architecture, or it is a whole scene in the native

idiom heightened into virtuosity. For this was no ordinary writer for the harpsichord, but, as we have said, the finest executant until the coming of Liszt. The temptation is to prolong this Spanish scene, but the limits of Scarlatti's life are nearly fulfilled.

xi

Return to Naples

*

WHEN HIS PATRON, THE PRINCE OF THE ASTU-
rias, came to the throne as Fernando VI, Scarlatti was already more than sixty years of age.
He missed, indeed, that strange episode at the
death of the Infanta Barbara when Fernando
wandered, unshaven and unwashed, in his
nightgown about the park. Soon after this, in
1759, the King died; but already, in 1754, having accomplished a quarter of a century of
service, Scarlatti had applied for leave to return
home to Naples. He arrived there just before
his seventieth birthday, and had come home pal-
pably to die. His end was a little delayed, for his
death is reported three years later, in 1757. He
would be aged seventy-two at that time.

Return to Naples

With the return of Scarlatti from Spain to Naples a great accumulation of his manuscripts must have been transferred, and then dispersed. What his fame may have been, after twenty-five years of virtual exile, it is difficult to know. The possession of one of the most famous names in Neapolitan music must have guarded him from oblivion in his lifetime. And, also, such close association with the greatest singers of the Neapolitan school must have kept his memory alive in Naples. But, in fact, he was too celebrated as the finest player in Italy and one of her most ingenious composers to be thus easily forgotten. During that twenty-five years he probably returned more than once to Naples, since, as we have seen, it was evidently not difficult for him to obtain leave to go as far afield as Dublin. His celebrity, therefore, we may safely assume, was kept alive during his absence.

At this point, for the last time, Dr. Burney comes to rescue our ignorance. This is through his meeting in Vienna, in 1774, with Dr. L'Augier, one of the principal physicians to the Imperial Court, and an ardent amateur of music. 'In spite of uncommon corpulency, he possessed a most active and cultivated mind.' Dr. Burney says that among his other acquirements he had heard national melody in all parts of the world with philosophical ears. It is Dr. L'Augier who informed Dr. Burney of the extent to which Scarlatti had been influenced in Spain by the music of the people. He is described by Dr. Burney as a living history of modern music. 'In Spain', we continue to quote from the learned Englishman, 'he was intimately acquainted with Domenico Scarlatti, who, at seventy-three, composed for him a great number of harpsichord lessons which he now possesses, and of which he favoured me with copies. The book in which they are transcribed contains forty-two pieces, among which are several slow movements; and of all these, I, who have been a collector of Scarlatti's compositions all my life, had never seen more than three or four. They were composed in 1756,[1] when Scarlatti was too fat to cross his hands as

[1] In 1756, Scarlatti was seventy-one, not seventy-three years of age. Dr. Burney was mistaken as to his age.

he used to do, so that these are not so difficult, as his more juvenile works, which were made for his scholar and patroness, the late Queen of Spain, when Princess of the Asturias.

'Scarlatti frequently told M. L'Augier, that he was sensible he had broken through all the rules of composition in his lessons; but asked if his deviation from these rules offended the ear? and, upon being answered in the negative, he said, that he thought there was scarce any other rule, worth the attention of a man of genius, than that of not displeasing the only sense of which music is the object.

'There are many passages in Scarlatti's pieces in which he imitated the melody of tunes sung by carriers, muleteers, and common people. He used to say that the music of Alberti, and of several other modern composers, did not in the execution want a harpsichord, as it might be equally well, or perhaps, better expressed by any other instrument; but, as nature had given him ten fingers, and as his instrument had employment for them all, he saw no reason why he should not use them.'

Return to Naples

This passage from Dr. Burney concludes what is practically the only first-hand account of Scarlatti that has come down to us. And, apart from its direct interest, it is of importance as showing the position in which Scarlatti was regarded by the authoritative opinion of the time. It is plain that Dr. Burney considered him to be one of the chief glories of Italian music. But music was soon to depart from Italy. Her predominance in opera lingered to a much later date than her excellence in instrumental music. Not much more than ten years after the death of Scarlatti the most eminent composer in Europe was not an Italian, but Haydn. Already, in Scarlatti's lifetime, the two great composers who were born in the same year as himself, Bach and Handel, were to bring on the collapse of Italian and the predominance of German music. The future neglect of Scarlatti was, therefore, a foregone conclusion, though he is in the curiously isolated position of being the only composer of the school of Naples whose name is familiar, or whose works are immediately recognised by the average concert-goer.

Return to Naples

So much excellent music was scrapped and thrown aside at the new discoveries and inventions of a later school. This was the fate of the school of Naples.

But, in the person of their one survivor, it should be possible to resume a few traits of that lost excellence. When Dr. Burney tells us that he went to Naples for the pleasure of its music, and then ascribes to Neapolitan music just those qualities of fire, of rapidity, of humour, that are our primary if superficial reaction to Scarlatti, we must be right in assuming that what was typical in the one composer applied to the whole body of which he was a member. His father, Alessandro Scarlatti, was the greatest of the Neapolitan composers: it is hardly likely that his son is the least representative of all that vast progeny. And its last paragons, the fruits of its decadence, should show in decay the over-ripening of the same characteristics. This is proved in Cimarosa and Paesiello, in whom rapidity has become quick but meaningless, force has degenerated into sweetness, and invention become patter and breathless enunciation. If humour and rapidity made one side of the Neapolitan genius, its other length of ornament, as exampled in the singing of the Castrati, is matched by the technical resource, the expert handling, which play so remarkable a part in the music of Scarlatti. For his music is one of the small things of the world, supremely well done. Its perfections are worn lightly, in just the air that he intended.

xii

Epilogue

★

MUSIC CAN MEAN ANYTHING TO ANYBODY (THIS
is the greatest of its prerogatives): but to one
person, at least, the music of Scarlatti differs in
essentials from all other music of the keyboard.
If this, perhaps solitary, opinion may be allowed a hearing the difference lies in that it
is inhabited music. The piano sonatas of Beethoven portray the conflicts of the soul; and, on
occasion, it may be thought, of a soul more
simple than that of Beethoven. By contrast,
Chopin is inhabited, but only by himself and
his various shades, in poses of gallantry or disillusionment. Perhaps it is music of his personality more than inhabited music! Delacroix was
only right in saying that no person like Chopin

had ever existed before, and that everything about him, his music, his appearance, his playing, were an integral part of this abnormal presentation. Schumann seems (still to this same solitary opinion) as the artist of the whole romantic age who most nearly achieved reality —reality, in that classical sense of true counterfeit. Poetry is all but transmuted by the heat of the crucible, so that the music becomes an experience in terms of poetry. If the Arabesque of Schumann is not a walk by the edge of a cornfield, then imagery is not an art of the senses. The music of Schumann is most essentially inhabited by beings, but seldom by more than one, and never by more than two. Do we not know enough of Schumann's character to be certain that this is true?

Mozart, in contrast to this, and in order to return nearer to Scarlatti, seems to be a composer whose purpose is always misinterpreted in his piano music. His works for the piano (for the piano concertos are a world in themselves which may be preferred in their entirety to his symphonies) must not be searched for Tartarean landscapes, or deep resolutions of the will. Apart from the four great Fantasias, and a few kindred works, it is surely right to look upon Mozart's piano compositions as his wanderings into an ideal world. This would, of necessity, be a world of deeper sensibility than that of Beethoven, lit by a more poetical imagination, and portrayed by his extraordinary faculty for extempore poetry into distances which lead along new directions upon the breath of inspiration. The beauty of his second subjects is, surely, only to be explained by the assumption that they are in the nature of a poetical extemporisation. To take one of the loveliest of all Mozart's works, the exquisite air which appears in the middle of the clarinet-quintet (first movement), cannot have been, to the mind at least of a humble poet, anything else except the sudden afflatus, the inexplicable accession of poetry. If this is proved in one of the more important of his instrumental works, it is all the more to be expected in his solitary imaginings, in works in which we are alone with Mozart and the direct prey, therefore, to his imagination. But, to tell the truth, the endless beauty of these apparently simple works is one of the miracles of art. What their inspiration may have been it is impossible to conceive; and Mozart, himself, admits this. 'When I am, as it were, completely myself, entirely alone and of good cheer—say, travelling in a carriage, or walking after a good meal, or during the night when I cannot sleep; it is on such occasions that my ideas flow best and most abundantly. Whence and how they come I know not; nor can I force them.' It is hopeless to attempt any explanation of these things. Their purpose, of enchantment, is more easily understood; and surely this was never so well achieved as when Keats describes himself as 'kept awake, as if by a tune of Mozart's'.[1] Such should be the haunting effect of these experiences of loveliness, though seldom have they had such a breast to cling to.

Even when Mozart does not touch the sub-

[1]In a letter to his brother, of 29th October, 1818. Actually it was Mrs. ——, an 'East-Indian', the thought of whom kept Keats awake and provoked this comparison.

lime heights of his art in the more slight of his piano works, his sense of shape and the filigree delicacy of his ornamentation raise the work on to a level of enchantment. At such moments it is, perhaps, not inappropriate to compare the effects to those of the most graceful stucco decoration. In these, he is the most accomplished of all the workers in rococo, and those who know the achievements of this delicate art in Austria and Southern Germany will admit that to say this is no derogation of Mozart in his lesser works. These arabesques impel admiration by the nice adjustment of their angle. Their trills and flourishes are inimitable—but the music is uninhabited.

If we return, now, to Scarlatti the difference dawns on us immediately. His music is, in comparison, as inhabited as a drawing by George Cruikshank. Perhaps we can define the difference still farther by another illustration in poetry. The poetry of Keats and Shelley is unpeopled. The poetry of Alexander Pope, by contrast, is alive with figures. *The Rape of the Lock* is the instant breath of contemporary

[135]

time. The incredible delicacy of its texture is
not torn by the admission of figures into that
gossamer world. Nor have those inhabitants any
shame of the moment in which they are living:
they appear perfectly contented and at ease in
their environment. There is nothing of nostalgia or discontentment in them. In Keats and
Shelley the age of complaint has already begun.
Even in *The Dunciad,* Pope is not so much
grumbling at the stupidity of his fellow men as
upbraiding them for their ignorance in what he
considered, obviously, to be an age of knowledge. It is not, perhaps, invidious to see a simi-
larity between Alexander Pope and Scarlatti.
The bustle and stir of their subjects, but, above
all, their possession of a caustic and sinister wit,
puts them into a division of mind in which we
must not expect to find Mozart, or Bach, or
Handel, as their companions. Both Alexander
Pope and Scarlatti, we may feel sure, preferred
the company of those who lived in towns. Pope
was, most particularly, the product of London:
Scarlatti was, more than all else, the Neapolitan. He had, even, the alert nerves of someone

who is used to traffic. No one who has passed his life in the country could have written the music of Scarlatti. He has no time to waste, and makes his points as sharply and rapidly as a jazz composer. The character of each separate piece is discernible from the start, even if it is the certainty that a surprise is coming. Speaking in terms of the nerves, of the sensibilities, Scarlatti is thinner and more rapid than Haydn; not broad-shouldered, with no peasant blood, honest more from education than from instinct, more dry and caustic in his wit. Haydn, we are told, and we may easily believe it, used to construct little contrivances of fire-irons, of books, of little pieces of furniture, making little houses and scenes out of such imaginary bricks and mortar in order to inspire and amuse himself. But the mind of Scarlatti will have been already stored with incident; he was under no necessity to invent, for his mental processes consisted in the transference of his direct observations into terms of music.

Haydn, in the andante of the *Clock* symphony, provides us with a perfect illustration of his own system. This is a construction as complete in itself as a fairy story. And it takes much less time in the telling than *Cinderella* or *The Sleeping Beauty*. The atmosphere of this piece of music is so finished, or, by extending that word, so furnished, that we might say even the cupboards are full. The cupboards are full; and, as well as the chiming of the different clocks, there is a cage of birds, and a saucer of milk for the cat. But, then, the kitchen is just as likely to drop its domestic tidiness and change into a high, empty room full of nothing but clocks, with tall doors in pairs along the walls, and no notion who may open them and come into the room. But nothing is sinister: it is only that everyone is asleep, leaving the mice to play and the clocks to tick. And so this extraordinary piece comes to an end, and we are left with the sensation of having travelled into the past, but found everyone asleep. The clocks are ticking and the inhabitants may wake again. The illusion of life is given by the very fact of its omission. It is just because the clocks are still ticking that their hearts must be beating and their bodies breathing. The purpose, then, of this visit to deserted rooms is to make a safe departure without waking the inmates, and the accomplishment of this leaves the riddle unanswered. The terrible question has not even been broached. It is, therefore, somewhat in the nature of a dream about dead friends. One is sorry for the dream to end, but glad that it finished without the posing of any awkward questions; and, all the time, that comforting voice which is ever by one's side in a pleasant dream and which is personified in the tone of this music, tells one not to worry and to enjoy it while it lasts.

The *Clock* symphony is the best example of Haydn in that vein in which Dr. Burney so admired him. In fact, the nearer he comes to Beethoven, but Dr. Burney could not know this, the less strongly does his own character emerge. It is Haydn, who is Haydn, whom we admire: not the Haydn who was precursor to Beethoven. Of all the composers of his lifetime Dr. Burney seems to have most admired Scarlatti and Haydn: it is when they approached each other that he was most content with either. The *Clock* symphony is certainly an instance in which Scarlatti and Haydn are not far removed from each other; but their attack, we have tried to suggest, was of an entirely different nature. We may put further stress upon this by the insistence that their habits of work must have been diametrically opposed. Haydn was in the habit of working for five or six hours of every day of his life. His habits were regular in the extreme, as is proved by the vast mass of his accomplishment. It is certain that he was a person of intensely punctual disposition, sitting down to work, every day, at exactly the same hour. We may imagine that his hours of rest were regulated in exactly the same way. No one who appreciates Haydn can think of him finishing a work in the heat and fury of inspiration. His was not the method of Berlioz, who would write nothing for months and then complete everything in a few days. Haydn was a slow worker, a person of steady inspiration, accomplishing his projects at his own deliberate pace. Scarlatti, with his essentially Latin temperament, will have worked more upon the system of Berlioz.

Epilogue

But the neat conciseness of his shape, compared with the Babylonian schemes of that unruly genius, did not call for such strenuous exertions on his part. It seems probable that his sonatas were written with extreme rapidity[1] and worked over with meticulous care. And from what we know of other artists with the same disposition of nerves, one may think that he must have written them in batches of several at a time. Many of them represent different aspects, or solutions, of the same problem, attacked from different angles.

Let us try, then, to build up his temperament in the light of what we know of his music and his surroundings. He was a Latin, a Neapolitan, and more probably a Sicilian. He was a native of the largest town in Italy, and, until he was forty-five years old, if he was not living in Naples he was residing in Rome, which was the capital of the arts. His father was the most

[1] It is said that in all the five hundred and forty-five sonatas of the complete edition of Scarlatti, only eighty-three have andantes or adagio movements. The rest are all rapidity and speed. This is most characteristic of their author.

[141]

Epilogue

famous musician in Italy; while, at Naples, he was in the midst of the most numerous school of musicians known to history. German music, even in its height of fame, is a mere handful of names compared to the school of Naples. He inherited his talent and brought it to early perfection. Before he was twenty-five years of age he was the finest virtuoso in Italy. We have tried to prove that in Rome and at Naples there was a large society of amateurs and of other artists who were interested in music. Vienna, in the time of Mozart or of Beethoven, was much smaller a town than Naples. It had no tradition of the arts. It was not Italian. Music was to Naples what painting was to Venice: it was the renown and fame of that Southern city.

For twenty years, after this, Scarlatti had the leisure to compose an extraordinary number of pieces for his instrument. A space of twenty years is sufficient time for any artist with energy to accumulate an imposing mass of material. It is as long by itself as the entire working life of Chopin. But, more than that he was an Italian, we must emphasise the point that Scarlatti was

Epilogue

a Neapolitan. He portrays for us the animation of a great city; and this is the town where gesture almost takes the place of language. These are not the burghers of Halle or Eisenach: they are inhabitants of a town of classical origin with an active volcano outside their doors. There is seldom a fall of snow, while the heats of summer necessitate the siesta. This, in itself, is an interruption to regular hours. His music represents the workings of the quickest race of brains. And by the very limitations of his art Scarlatti was absolved from wasting his energies on religious themes. This had been the bane of Italian art of all and every description, throughout its history. Its absence, in his music, is one of its delights.

We, then, see him, at forty-five years of age, accepting an appointment which withdrew him altogether from popular fame. The circumstances of this, while they gave him every opportunity of continuing his work, are unrivalled in picturesqueness and improbability. We have endeavoured to show that music, far from being isolated at the Court of Spain, and

[143]

only represented by his person, was, in actual
fact, of daily incidence, and the best thing of its
kind procurable by money. During the twenty-
five years that he passed in Spain, it is not to be
wondered at if he became tinged, to some extent, with the Iberian character. No one can
pass a quarter of a century in a foreign land and
not be affected by the transplantation. In dealing with a person of Scarlatti's lively intelligence, it would be still more peculiar were
Spain to pass over him and leave no marks of its
strong and bitter blood. Even to-day it has more
individuality than any land in Europe: in the
early part of the eighteenth century it was a
world apart and content with itself. That book
of fabulous intent, Mme. d'Aulnoy's *Voyage en
Espagne*, gives us a picture of Spain that we
know is not exaggerated, even if it is strange.
For Spain will not have changed much between
1660 and 1729; and even if it is true that Mme.
d'Aulnoy never went there and only compiled
her book from the accounts of her daughter and
sister, it only doubles the evidence and does not
alter the facts. If it be a masterpiece of imagina-

tion, let it stand and do not contradict it! But all the circumstances point to its veracity. In any case, the authoress of those famous fairy stories can have thought of nothing more fantastic and improbable than the true state of affairs, sixty years later, at the Spanish Court. The names of Farinelli and Egizziello are a perpetual reminder of this, while the addition of Domenico Scarlatti to their company steadies that strangeness with its certainty of touch. The poor, mad Kings and Queens lose something of their pathos by these proofs of their extreme normality and their exquisite taste. João V is shown as more sensible than a dictator who prepares for war, and money given to music is better spent than money gone on battleships. Golden coaches, or silver plate, or palaces built for a single night, all these extravagances have both an argument, and a modern counterpart more easily confuted.

The brief aftermath to Scarlatti's life, when he returned to Naples to die, must have seemed like a return to reason, with the enchantment gone. It is to be hoped, and may be surmised, that he was in circumstances of affluence after so considerable an absence. In all probability he was given a generous pension, for his patrons, Fernando and Barbara, did not die, we must remember, until five years after Scarlatti's return to Naples. In fact, they outlived their musician. On the other hand, we are told that Scarlatti was a gambler, that his family were reduced to destitution, and that they had to be rescued by the generosity of his old friend Farinelli.

Naples was, by now, a kingdom ruled over by Carlos III, the half-brother of Fernando. His reign may be described as the golden age of Naples. The city flourished, as never before, and great works such as the building of Caserta were undertaken. This project of Roman magnificence, the last work of slaves,[1] was begun, in fact, in 1752, just before the return of Scarlatti to Naples. Carlos III was Heir to the Spanish

[1]In 1765, there were employed at Caserta 165 Turkish slaves, and 160 baptised slaves, who were better treated than the others. They worked very badly, were always trying to escape, and 250 soldiers had to guard them.— Lalande, *Voyage en Italie*, vol. vi, p. 121.

Throne, so that the political illusion in which Scarlatti's last years were spent was one of Spanish dominion—historically, the greatest power in Europe. Most of Scarlatti's life had been passed in Spanish service; and, once and for all, there is this last opportunity to emphasise Spain and The Two Sicilies as his background. He was the subject of this double-kingdom, just as much as Goya was the subject of Carlos IV or Fernando VII, his contemporary Kings of Spain. It is a vanished kingdom, but it had its existence as surely as the lost lands of Poland or Burgundy.

For the last moment let us listen to those neat and rapid hands. No music, before or since, has been so inhabited by character. And this peculiar talent is only magnified in scope by its seclusion in the haunted precincts of that palace. All normal life, and all the stir and excitement of ordinary mortals, passed into the possession of this ghostly King and his dwarf Queen. The flowering of daily life in that noisy city of the South filled the stillness. For the melancholic silence must be broken, if only by the chiming

Epilogue

of musical clocks. When we listen to the music of Domenico Scarlatti we must imagine it interrupted by those exotic tones, and followed by the warblings of Farinelli and Egizziello. The patrons of Scarlatti were more extraordinary phantoms of over-breeding than have ever disturbed naturalist or botanist. This race of ghostly monsters lived in an isolation, as we have said, comparable to the survival of a race of dinosaurs. And they were the gluttons of music. It was their only defence against melancholia.

Such, in short, was the life of this great composer and executant, as we have painted him in his different phases. For all the smallness of his compass he remains one of the most important figures in musical art. There are but few things, in all of the arts, done to such perfection and worked to so bewildering a variety out of such simple material. In this respect, it is only possible to compare Domenico Scarlatti with Chopin; and if we long for a less troubled existence we prefer Scarlatti, and find him living in a world, not occupied exclusively by himself and his aspirations and disappointments, but

Epilogue

crowded with figures, enlivened with living architecture, lit with tradition, and enlarged, finally, into a land of magical opportunity, where his own skill and poetry were matched as they have seldom been in the annals of chance. It was only a step, or a short sea-voyage, from the magic of his own music to the enchanted palace.

xiii

Postscript

★

SOME PARTS OF THIS POSTSCRIPT MAY SEEM TO speak of far-off things, but I hope to prove that they have a near contingency to my subject. There is a division of mankind, among whom I include myself, for whom Scarlatti has possessed an unique fascination from the very first contact with his music. An unmistakable personality, instantly recognised, is the first and most salient characteristic of Scarlatti; and many people, like myself, could testify to the truth of this from the earliest memories of their childhood. Speaking for myself, I learned to recognise Scarlatti before I was certain of Mozart. It is difficult exactly to describe his tell-tale features, but they consist, more than anything else,

[151]

in the alliance of rapidity and humour. It is
Scarlatti, and could be none other, when these
qualities have their play.

An early interest in his music was fortified,
before I was twenty years old, by what seemed
to be the unbelievable grace and rapidity of
Diaghilev's company in *Le donne di buon umore*,
and by many unforgettable evenings, when,
among a host of other things, his sonatas were
played upon the harpsichord, as they can seldom
have been played since his death, by the great
artist to whom this book is dedicated. It became,
then, a fascination to attempt to fill the long
blanks in the little that is known of his life;
while the fact that this was passed in surroundings that appealed to me for so many other
reasons had the effect of doubling my interest in
him. But the link made by Scarlatti with these
other interests was twofold; that he is the only
Italian of the classical school whose music can be
said in any sense to have survived to our day,
and that, for this period, he is the fusion of
Southern Italy and Spain. This was a conjunction of which there is only one other instance in

the arts of the time. The person in question was Luca Giordano. This is not the place in which to discuss his works; but those who see his frescoes on the staircase at the Escurial and on the ceiling of the sacristy in Toledo Cathedral will come away from Spain with revised ideas as to his merits as a painter. The life of Scarlatti, as regards the circumstances of his employment, presents something of a parallel, but a much extended one, to that of this neglected artist. But, here again, the personal reasons that have prompted this interest deserve an explanation.

To a person who has passed a great deal of his life in Italy, the other alternative, of Spain, has a peculiar and understandable fascination. This may have begun, so far as I am concerned, on a certain day in Venice, in 1907 or 1908, when I witnessed on the Grand Canal a scene that I shall never be able to forget. The floating ease of an afternoon spent in a gondola was enlivened, of a sudden, by much noise and stir coming from the water-gate of a near-by palace, the Palazzo Loredan. The iron gates were thrown open, a wooden gangway was put down, and an

immensely tall old man with a square white
beard, dressed, if I remember right, in black,
but wearing, certainly, an immense black som-
brero, came down the steps and, leaning on the
arm of a little black page, crossed the plank into
a waiting gondola. The negro page followed
him and stood in the bows of the boat, while six
gondoliers in magnificent liveries lifted their
painted oars, in stripes of red and yellow, and in
an instant the gondola slid out from the shadows
into the sunlight and was gone. To our enquiries, we were told that this was the Pretender to the Throne of Spain. It was, in fact,
the embarcation of Don Carlos.

The effect of this romantic vision was to
waken a lively interest in Spain, in Spanish history, and in the woes of that family who are, in
themselves, the history of Spain. It was to be
many years before I went to Spain; but, typi-
cally enough, the afternoon of my very first day
in Madrid, after a morning spent in the Prado
making acquaintance with Velasquez and with
Goya, I went to a bull-fight, and there, sitting
in a box and being cheered by the crowd and

saluted by the matadors, in a high mantilla that did not hide her aquiline features, was the living embodiment of a figure from the great group of of the Royal Family by Goya. This was the Infanta Isabella, aunt of King Alfonso, who attended every bull-fight and lived at La Granja, the palace that has been so often mentioned in these preceding pages. Her extraordinary appearance was like another vision from the past; and the fact that she had been married to the Count of Girgenti, brother of the last King of The Two Sicilies, gave her additional interest in my eyes.

But the fortunes of the dispossessed branch of this family, who, being directly descended in the male line from the Kings and Queens mentioned in this book, will have preserved their feudal or heraldic features in undiminished peculiarity, give an extraordinary glamour to everything that concerns Don Carlos. He died a year or two after my view of him in Venice, and his son, Don Jaime, died in Paris, two years ago, after a reconciliation with King Alfonso. The only male member of that branch of the family now alive is Don Alfonso Carlos, the younger brother of Don Carlos. More of European history runs in his veins than in those of any other person living, so that it is impossible to think of this old gentleman, now in his eighty-sixth year, otherwise than in a halo of romance. And it is, perhaps, because no tribute has been paid to him by any other English author that the need is more pressing and its backward contingency more visible, being in himself so easy a connection with Felipe V and Fernando VI, or, for the matter of that, with Charles V and with Louis XIV.

He was born in London in 1849, and is still living in Austria, in his castle at Ebenzweier, or else at Frohsdorf, which was inherited from his uncle, the Comte de Chambord, last of the French Bourbons. An Austrian friend of mine, who lives near Ebenzweier, has described to me the romantic impression made upon him, as a child, by the sight of Don Alfonso Carlos riding with his wife, Donna Maria de las Nieves. Two horsemen in liveries of scarlet and gold, the colours of Spain, preceded them. Then came

Postscript

Don Alfonso, in a tall top-hat, wearing long black trousers and golden spurs, mounted on a black horse; while Donna Maria de las Nieves rode a snow-white charger by his side. Two more horsemen, in scarlet and gold, rode behind. This very summer, while in the neighbourhood, I visited Ebenzweier in the hopes of catching a glimpse of this romantic couple, though old age, and, it may be feared, poverty, have altered their mode of life, and they no longer go out riding, as formerly. Unfortunately they were away from Ebenzweier at the time of my visit, so that my curiosity to have seen them remains unsatisfied. I had to be content, while buying post-cards in the village shop, to be told how much they were beloved by the villagers, and that when in residence they take a walk together, 'like young children', while their negress, 'Frau Poppetta', walks respectfully behind, in attendance upon them.

The interest attaching to this romantic pair of survivors has been enhanced to an extraordinary degree by the publication, in 1934, of the first volume of the memoirs of Donna

Postscript

Maria de las Nieves.[1] These concern the Second Carlist War of 1872-76, in which she played a prominent part. The Infanta Maria de las Nieves is, in herself, scarcely less remarkable from point of descent than her husband, being the eldest of the six daughters of the Pretender Dom Miguel of Portugal, who was the direct male descendant of Dom João V. The fact that the name of Dom Miguel, once of monotonous frequency in European affairs, should scarcely appear at all in European politics after 1834, the year in which he was expelled from Portugal, makes it scarcely credible that all six of his daughters, once famous for their beauty, should be still alive. At the time of the outbreak of the Second Carlist War Donna Maria de las Nieves was not twenty years of age, but she proceeded at once to Spain and distinguished herself at the head of her husband's army. His brother, Don Carlos, commanded the main force, while smaller commands were given to himself and

[1]*Mis Memorias*, by Maria de las Nieves de Bragança y de Borbón, Madrid, Espasa-Calpe, 1934. A second volume of these memoirs is to appear later.

Postscript

to the Count of Caserta, brother of the last King
of The Two Sicilies, who survived till last year.
Donna Maria de las Nieves was in the fore-
front of every battle, urging on the troops from
her white charger. She was a born soldier. In
fact, her memoirs are the recollections of a
general, and are scarcely credible as those of a
girl of twenty.

All lovers of romance and of lost causes will be
moved by the thought of this book of memoirs published by this old Infanta of eighty-two
years of age, no less than sixty years after the
campaign in which she took part. There were
moments when it seemed as if success would
come to the Carlists. Nearly the whole of Nor-
thern Spain was in their hands, and their army,
divided into regiments of Basques and of
Zouaves, was animated with superb spirit and
bravery by the example of the Infanta, who
shared the hardships of the field with her troops
and appeared, daily, on horseback, on her white
charger. She wore uniform, and sported a kind
of Zouave jacket lined with astrakhan. Her tunic
was covered with medals, she carried a gilt

riding-switch, and her head-dress was a bright red Basque bonnet, or béret, with a long gilded tassel.

The results of this protracted war were in doubt for some two years, at least, but in the end it was evident to all that the Carlists were fighting for a lost cause. Their numbers dwindled, and, at last, they had to own defeat; and Don Carlos, with his brother Don Alfonso Carlos and the Infanta, had to cross the frontier into France, sooner than surrender to the forces of Alfonso XII. They travelled straight from the last battlefield, by the first train they could reach, to London, and arrived at Brown's Hotel, in Dover Street, still wearing their stained and dusty uniforms, and carrying the marks of battle upon them.

Thus ended the Second Carlist War, and from that day till this, over a period of sixty years, Don Alfonso Carlos and Donna Maria de las Nieves have never returned to Spain. The publication of this book is as if we had a full-length account of 1745 written by the Pretender himself, and published sixty years after-

[160]

wards, in 1805. During this immense interval
they have lived almost entirely in Austria, and
chiefly at Ebenzweier, where the arms of
France and Spain can be seen over the gate of
their castle. The second and third generation of
the Spanish servants who followed them from
Spain live in the surrounding houses, forming
a little Spanish colony; but they can no longer
speak their native tongue.

In addition to this castle, Don Alfonso Carlos
owns the castle of Frohsdorf, which he inherited
from his nephew, Don Jaime. This came to
them, as we have said, from the Comte de
Chambord. There, that last of the French Bourbons had lived in the care of servants from the
Tuileries, who had left that palace in 1830 in
the train of Charles X, and accompanied him
on his leisurely journey with the Guard to the
French coast, to Holyrood, and eventually to
Graz, in Austria, where he died. They had then
entered the service of his grandson, the Comte
de Chambord (Henri V). It is said that these
servants, who possessed curious, mediaeval sur-
names, had lived for generations and, indeed,

for centuries in the Tuileries, and that they spoke a dialect, or patois, of mediaeval French. The household of the Comte de Chambord was organised on traditional lines, with food-tasters, *officiers de la bouche*, and so forth, and the food was carried into the dining-room locked in immense silver dishes. A few of the descendants of these same servants are still at Frohsdorf, in the service of Don Alfonso Carlos, but, equally with his Spanish retainers, have forgotten the use of their own language.

It is to be hoped that these few details convey something of the extraordinary interest that attaches to this old gentleman, who should, legally, be King of France as well as King of Spain. There is ever a sense of melancholy romance where a Pretender is concerned. Amateur Jacobites, and their number is legion from Queen Victoria downwards, will have sympathy with this assertion. It is this that invests the Stuarts with their halo of romance; and, where the arts are concerned, it is this that gives the scenes of the false Dmitri, in *Boris Godunov*, their extraordinary glamour. Jacobites will share the au-

Postscript

thor's interest in the brothers Sobieski Stuart,
and the pathos of their pretensions; but this interest quickens into something more than that
where persons of such an authentic legendary
importance as Don Alfonso Carlos are concerned. His very surname, Bourbon-Hapsburg-
d'Este, bespeaks the history of Europe; and
Donna Maria de las Nieves cannot be said to be
any less romantic as a figure for our contemplation. While they are alive they deserve, at least,
the tribute of this little attention.

In their persons, where many histories will
come only too soon to their natural conclusion,
we see the heraldic extinction of so many things
that have come down to us, unbroken, out of a
distant past. The very name Don Carlos was an
intoxication, an inebriation of romance, when
it was first heard and its owner seen, on that
afternoon, long ago, in Venice. His brother,
with whom we have dealt at greater length because he is still alive, is the direct male descendant, by primogeniture, of Felipe V, the patron
of Scarlatti. The Infanta Maria de las Nieves, his
wife, is the direct descendant of Dom João V,

Postscript

the father of the Infanta Barbara, the scholar and pupil of Scarlatti. The sight of Don Carlos gave the author his first interest in Spain; while that prince's brother and wife are direct descendants of the two families who constituted the history of Spain and Portugal during the eighteenth century. Twenty-five years were spent by Domenico Scarlatti in the service of a King of Spain who was the victim of melancholia. Perhaps, therefore, these remarks upon the last legal and titular male descendant of the Spanish Bourbons are in no unsuitable place as conclusion to the history of an individual who was closely concerned with them over so long a period. No history, for instance, that dealt with James II of England would end inappropriately with a few remarks upon the melancholy and romantic fate of his descendants. It is, in fact, without scruple that I have added this epilogue of Spanish history to a book dealing so largely in the personalities of an earlier period. It is in the certainty that it will interest at least a few readers who find their interest in Scarlatti augmented by the peculiar and romantic circumstances of his employment. In the life of Scarlatti all, or nearly all, is mystery; and, in the opinion of the author, one side at any rate of the history with which he was concerned, and in which he lived, will not reach to its natural conclusion until this last representative of its tragedy is no longer in our midst. Then, and then only, will that phase be extinguished.

Domenico Scarlatti brought his lively and inhabited music to be the solace of Fernando and Barbara, who, from their melancholy, were as constantly exiled from the world of men and women as their descendants are exiled from Spain. But this music can perform an identical service to ourselves by the easy rapidity with which it carries us back into his peculiar and unique world. There is no one else who is creator of the same scenes. It is no wonder that they had such an appeal to a King and Queen who lived on the edge, on the rim of sanity. For the marvel of Scarlatti is his balance. He travels at unheard-of speeds, creates an atmosphere in the flash of a second; he populates, as it were, the streets and squares, needing no

Postscript

more than a moment or two to complete his work.

And so the last words of this epilogue shall bring us back to these patrons of his maturity. All that there is of fact concerning his twenty-five years in Spain could be told in the space of two or three lines. If that sentence, or two, has been needlessly expanded we must crave the reader's indulgence. Our excuse is in the interest that attaches to every possibility and all the personalities of that long employment. It is only by attempting this that the blank canvas of his life can be completed. Otherwise, there would be no more than a few dates to record, and all the rest of his life would be mystery and silence.

Author's Note

★

IN THE PREPARATION OF THIS BOOK IT WOULD be superfluous to mention the author's indebtedness to articles in Grove's *Dictionary of Music* and in the *Encyclopaedia Britannica*. Dr. Burney has been the other most frequently consulted authority. The author's special gratitude to Professor E. J. Dent must, also, be stated. His life of *Alessandro Scarlatti* (London, 1905), the father of Domenico, is a mine of information respecting the Neapolitan school of composers; and he has been kind enough, also, to inform the author upon one or two points of importance. The interesting question of Scarlatti's utilisation of Spanish themes is discussed in Mr. J. B. Trend's book upon *Manuel de Falla* (New York, 1929), and in a couple of articles in *Music and Letters* for April 1922, and in the

Author's Note

Musical Quarterly for 1927. This question was apparently first raised by the composer Joaquin Nin; but the dimensions of the problem are very far from exhausted, and much work remains to be done upon this subject. Articles upon Scarlatti by Malipiero and by Alessandro Longo have, also, been consulted; but, generally speaking, there is a remarkable absence of both information and of written criticism regarding Scarlatti. There is an interesting article upon the two Scarlattis by Philip Radcliffe in *The Heritage of Music*, Volume II, Oxford University Press, 1934. Finally, it should be stated that where the names Fernando and Ferdinando appear in these pages, it is because Fernando is the Spanish, and Ferdinando the Italian, form of that name. There were, for example, Fernando VII of Spain and Ferdinando I of The Two Sicilies.